CONFESSIONS OF A CAFFEINATED CHRISTIAN

D0448480

CONFESSIONS OF A
CAFFEINATED CHRISTIAN

JOHN FISCHER

WIDE-AWAKE
AND NOT
ALONE

SALT**RIVER**™

AN IMPRINT OF
TYNDALE HOUSE PUBLISHERS, INC.

Visit Tyndale's exciting Web site at www.tyndale.com

TYNDALE is a registered trademark of Tyndale House Publishers, Inc.

Tyndale's quill logo is a trademark of Tyndale House Publishers, Inc.

SaltRiver and the *SaltRiver* logo are trademarks of Tyndale House Publishers, Inc.

Confessions of a Caffeinated Christian

Copyright © 2005 by John Fischer. All rights reserved.

Cover photo © by Rabel Design Project/Alamy. All rights reserved.

Chapter opener photographs taken by Luke Daab. Copyright 2005 by Tyndale House Publishers. All rights reserved.

Author photo copyright © 2004 by Tom Lamb. All rights reserved.

Cover design by Barry Smith

Interior design by Luke Daab

Unless otherwise indicated, all Scripture quotations are taken from the *Holy Bible,* New International Version®. NIV®. Copyright © 1973, 1978, 1984 by International Bible Society. Used by permission of Zondervan Publishing House. All rights reserved.

Scripture quotations marked KJV are taken from the *Holy Bible,* King James Version.

Library of Congress Cataloging-in-Publication Data

Fischer, John, Date.
Confessions of a caffeinated Christian : wide awake and not alone / John Fischer.
p. cm.
Includes bibliographical references.
ISBN 0-8423-8434-0 (sc)
1. Fischer, John, 1947- 2. Christian biography—United States. I. Title.
BR1725.F49A3 2005
277.3'0825'092—dc22   2004026297

Printed in the United States of America

09 08 07 06 05
5   4   3   2   1

SHALL WE MEET?

We haven't seen each other for a while.
Let's have a bonding experience over a great cup
of coffee and this book. . . .

Please meet me over a lively brew.

WHEN: .... AT: .... O'CLOCK

WHERE: ....

Call and let me know if you can come.
Here's my phone number:

....

Wide-awake to your reply,

CONTENTS

CHAPTER ONE
BLOWING
BUBBLES

I was born dead. This may not entirely account for my subsequent passion for coffee, but it may have something to do with it. I was the last of three children—a kind of afterthought—and I was prayed over to get here, or at least that's how my mother used to tell the story. I'm sure she embellished it quite a bit over the course of the thousands of times it was told, making me a sort of legend in my own mind. The story never got beyond the walls of my house—it wasn't that big of a story—but it's certain that if you ever visited my home when I was growing up, you would have heard about it within fifteen minutes of walking in the door.

It's the story of how I was born. I, of course, don't remember anything firsthand, but the legend goes that when I was delivered I wasn't breathing. That part was actually anticipated due to complications in my mother's pregnancy. In fact, the doctor had presumed one of us would not make it through the birthing experience. Since my mother was breathing fine at the moment of my birth, that wasn't good news for me. Believing I didn't have much of a chance, they put me aside and tended to my mother. That was when the doctor's wife started praying. (The doctor and his wife and my parents were best friends. They used to sing gospel songs in the kitchen while they did the dishes together. I often fell asleep listening to those songs.)

Sometime during her prayer I started blowing bubbles. It was a miracle, and I was considered the miracle baby. I'm still breathing today; my mother is not, but that doesn't have anything to do with my being born. I know that because she went on breathing for fifty years after that. My mother was a very dynamic lady, although she was a little taken with my birth story. She kept telling it because it was her story, and she was so happy that God had answered prayer. After hearing the story over and over, however, I began to think I was special, which meant that more was going to be expected of me someday. "God's going to use you for something big," my mother used to tell me.

I wish she hadn't told me that. I wish my mother had made me face the fact that I wasn't more special than anyone else. "Special" would have been fine as long as it was just something in the family—special to her and my dad, the people everyone should be special to—not a kind of "special" that made me think I was set apart from the rest of the pack.

But my mother kept the story going as a continual reminder: I was alive because God had big plans for me. Unfortunately, I took this the wrong way and became obnoxious, arrogant, and overbearing (my childhood friends told me this later in life). Things were never my fault. I was never wrong. I had answers for everything. And if others had a problem with me, it was only because they hadn't grasped how special I was yet.

* * *

The doctor and his wife were named Hugh and Frances. Frances was a demure, petite woman who somehow managed to birth five boys, all breathing. Our families were very close; we did everything together until I was about eight or nine and they moved away.

In addition to their home in San Marino, California, Frances and Hugh had a cabin in the mountains and acreage on ranch land somewhere near Lake Elsinore, where one summer we all put up a World War II Quonset hut (an odd metal building with a semicylindrical corrugated tin roof that was left over from the war). So it was trips to Lake Arrowhead for skiing in the winter and Lake Elsinore for hiking and murdering birds in the summer.

At least that's what I remember most about the ranch. That was where I shot my first bird with a BB gun—a little orange wren I winged while out "hunting" with Danny, my best friend among the brothers, and Hubert, the next oldest. When the bird fell, Hubert picked up the struggling creature and choked it to death with his fingers, despite my protests. I had to watch while the bird's eyes twitched and a drop of blood fell from its beak. Aiming at it, hitting it with a BB, and watching it flop out of a tree were fun. Watching it being choked to death was not fun at all. I brought the dead bird home that night in an empty milk carton and tried to get it to breathe. I even prayed over it like Frances had done over me, but I didn't get the same result. I had blown bubbles; the wren blew blood.

I always thought Hubert was a bully. He was older than Danny and me, and I never liked it when he hung out with us. Danny was older than me, too, but only by five months. He was small and slight like his mother, and he always used to say, "You may be bigger than me, John, but you'll never, ever be older than me." Over time, he has proven to be right about that.

I think Hubert got his bullying nature from his dad, who had a rough exterior. He rarely smiled, even when he was happy. Once five of us kids were jammed into the backseat of Hugh's Cadillac coming down the mountains when he got really mad at us for making too much noise. He turned around and yelled at us to shut up or he would pull over and leave us all on the side of the road. The ensuing shock silenced all of us in the backseat until he cleared his throat and spit out the window. If Hugh was trying to impress us with his tough-guy persona, it would have helped if the window had been rolled down. Five kids immediately froze in the backseat. For an instant the universe stopped as the green, stringy blob slowly oozed down the window. It was useless. The dam inevitably broke, sending us howling with laughter. We laughed until the car shook. It was one time I actually remember Hugh allowing a little smile to creep across his face.

I think I could have used a little more exposure to Hugh. I don't think he ever bought my birth story as being very different from any other birth. There's a way of looking at births that makes them all miracles, and he'd certainly seen a lot of them. To him, I wasn't that special—just another kid he had helped bring into the world.

✳ ✳ ✳

I have always had a thing for *Saturday Night Live*'s Church Lady. Not that I liked her or anything, just that I fully understood her. Especially her use of the word *special*. It was cathartic for me to watch someone on national TV make a big deal of being special—even when portrayed as a mockery of fundamentalism. *I must not be the only one with this problem,* I would tell myself. Why would Dana Carvey have picked this one thing to mock about conservative Christians if it wasn't something obvious to him and to his audience? "Well, isn't that special?"

was the Church Lady's favorite phrase. Apparently Christians have made a lot of people feel what I made my friends feel when I was growing up—that I was too good for them.

Years later as a husband and father, I was getting counsel from a psychologist when we delved into this whole idea of being special. I told him my mother's birth story—somewhat surprised that he hadn't heard it before, since he went to the same church my parents attended. When I got to the part about Frances praying and my bubble-blowing, he moved up to the edge of his chair, his face animated.

"John, do you know what that means?" he asked, full of anticipation. I didn't respond only because I knew what was coming next. He was going to say it meant I was special and God was expecting big things from me. So I stared at him, waiting for the obvious and wondering what he could possibly be so excited about.

"That means God wanted you to live!"

I sat there in stunned silence.

"That's it?" I finally said. "That's all?"

"Well, that's a pretty big deal," he said.

So that was it all along. God wanted me alive and breathing. He wanted *me*. I am alive, not because of what I did, or was going to do, or how I got here. I am alive, period, and suddenly that alone became a pretty big deal.

I could have kissed the psychologist. As it was, I rushed out of that session and called my wife. I couldn't even wait to get home to tell her.

"Guess what? God wants me to live! Isn't that great?"

In my imagination I embraced every person I passed in the hallway and on the way to my car. I suddenly felt connected with everyone I saw. They must be pretty special. God wanted them to live too.

CHAPTER TWO
BASEBALL
FOR ONE

I love coffee. I love it dark, oily, and with a burnt chestnut aftertaste. Starbucks' French Roast is my variety of choice. The beans have to be almost black and a little wet. Dry, brown beans do not make a coffee that interests me.

There is hardly anything I know better than my first cup of coffee in the morning. I know exactly how to brew it to my liking. I know how long the flavor will last in a thermal pot and at what point an insulated carafe loses its maximum effectiveness.

It has not always been this way. There was a time, say thirty years ago, when coffee was coffee. You could have it black or you could disguise it with cream and/or sugar, but those were the only options. Over the last thirty years, European influences have turned coffee drinking into an experience, and coffee drinkers have all become experts at how they like their coffee. People in their twenties grew up with these options. Little by little, I have been reeducated on the fine points of coffee.

We found out that if hot water drips over the grounds only once, the coffee has the best flavor. We discovered that grinding our own beans maximizes the intensity. We went through the grind-your-own-beans, tap-the-grounds-into-a-cone-filter, heat-up-the-water, and pour-it-slowly-over-the-grounds phase. And when we wanted only one cup of coffee, we could use small, one-cup cones to drip a few ounces of fresh coffee directly into our mug.

Then someone popularized the automatic drip coffeemaker. It heats the water and drips it slowly over the grounds, much as if you poured it yourself. Then we found out that the water made a big difference, so we started making our coffee with filtered water. Now a variety of machines brew coffee to our liking. The most sophisticated, upon cue from its internal timer, will grind beans, deliver the grounds to a basket, heat up the water, pour it over the basket, drip freshly brewed coffee into a thermal pot, and seal it until you take your first sip upon rising in the morning. I'm not sure I want to give up that much control over the process. I've found that ground Starbucks' French Roast, available at the supermarket, and a regular drip coffeemaker (I can pour the extra coffee into a thermal pot myself, thank you) meet my daily needs just fine.

Along with this new education came the rise of the coffee bistro. Now that we knew what a good cup of coffee was, we were willing to pay up to three dollars for such a thing, and even more for European versions of the drink with steamed milk added, as in cappuccinos and lattes. Soon the coffee "place" was born—a comfortable setting where "coffee" becomes more than a drink, it's an experience.

Now coffee is more than something to wake you up in the morning. It is a steaming mug to wrap your fingers around and use to turn your mind on. And a coffeehouse is a place to be with friends, or a place to be alone while still among "friends." Even if you don't know anybody and don't talk to anybody, you still feel as if you are with people who have the same love for coffee and enjoy the moment as much as you do.

In one of these places it's hard not to feel a little superior as I reflect and enjoy my coffee while everyone else rushes by. Of course, in a minute, I will join them and rush on myself, but for a while I am an observer. I have stepped off the moving walkway for a moment and can watch everyone else glide by.

It's one thing to do this once in a while in a coffee shop, but it's another thing to live your whole life separated from the flow. I trained myself early on to live in my own world. For a few things, like writing, that has been a good thing. For most everything else, such as living in relationship with family and community, it has been very bad.

My parents' house was on a street lined with Chinese elms and modest homes in San Gabriel, California, a half block from George Washington Elementary, where I attended kindergarten and all eight grades of grammar school. It was a straight shot out my front door, across the street, down the sidewalk, and through a gap in the fence to the playground. My house was so close I could walk home for lunch every day, and when I was home sick, I could hear the clamor of children on the playground at recess.

I still have a piece of that playground embedded in my nose. One day I fell headfirst off the handlebars of my brother's bike and ground my face into the asphalt. Hugh said he got as much out as he could, but I'd probably have some of it there the rest of my life. He was right. We all carry pieces of our childhood in our memories. I have some in my nose as well.

I lived so close to school that I used to kick the same rock back and forth, trying to beat my last record of least number of kicks necessary to get it to and from school.

I've always played little games like this by myself, most likely because I was the third child and separated from my nearest sibling by six years. I grew up in my own world. The most sophisticated of my solitary games was a realistic baseball game I came up with in my backyard.

I would throw a tennis ball as high as I could so it

would come down hard on the back half of the roof and then fly off in a random direction after landing on the roof's uneven wooden shingles. The rules were simple. Each throw was a batter, and I had to catch the ball to get that batter out. Failure to do so yielded a single, double, triple, or home run depending on where in the yard the ball landed. The totally erratic behavior of the tennis ball bouncing off the shingles of the roof is what made the game unpredictable enough to hold my attention. The ball could carom off the front edge of a shingle and become a screaming line drive that was impossible to reach; it could pop up like a lazy fly ball; it could hit the tree in the middle of the yard (I had to play the ball as it dropped through the branches); or it could hit a shingle just right and mysteriously propel itself over the wall behind our patio for a booming home run.

I played nine-inning games and kept a scorecard on every hitter on the home team, which was always the current version of the Los Angeles Dodgers'. I had my own stats on Maury Wills, Duke Snyder, Sandy Koufax, and their teammates. The games turned out to be incredibly realistic and full of subtle innuendo. I would have low-scoring games, high-scoring games, blowouts, ninth-inning comebacks—you name it. I could play like this for hours.

＊ ＊ ＊

I attended the school down the street for nine years, but I really wasn't there. Let me explain. Most kids have a life that revolves around family, neighborhood, and school. My life had one more element thrown in—church—and church played such a significant role that it eclipsed the other three. In addition, church was two cities away. Because my dad was the choir director, my mom taught Sunday school, and my older brother and sister were active in their respective youth groups, I developed my primary peer relationships at church. Even Danny and Hubert (the bird choker) attended our church, though they went to another school.

As a result, there wasn't one person who went to both my church and my school besides me. I lived a segregated life in two worlds that never met, and my place in these worlds was vastly different. In one world I was somebody; in the other I was nobody. In one I was thought of as a leader; in the other I was largely invisible. In one world I was confident; in the other I was intimidated. At church I was part of the "in" crowd; at school I was definitely "out."

My relationships with my peers at school were, at best, apprehensive. I learned to alternatively judge and envy them. Our brand of evangelicalism implied that people who didn't believe as we did were bad people with whom we had little in common, so I judged them. But they were also smart, attractive, talented people who knew how to have a good time, and for this I envied them.

To this day, I don't think I know how to have or be a friend very well. I grew up believing I was better than everybody in church (they weren't as "special" as me) and intimidated by everyone at school (I wasn't "in" like them). Yes, I was lonely, but I had my rock to kick and my backyard baseball to keep me happy. Looking back, I think I really wanted it that way.

My actual school-related memories are so limited I can count them on one hand. Tom Flory and I wore the same clothes to school every day for a few weeks in the first grade. Jane Parmalee was my second-grade girlfriend for a while. I ran a footrace to win the right to walk her home from school and play board games like Park and Shop on her back porch. Larry Sabin was my Ping-Pong nemesis after school. Beyond that, everything I remember about school is pretty faceless. At school, I was more of an observer than a participant—early training for my later coffee-shop experiences.

My most disengaging experience at George Washington Elementary was being excused from the school's "social dancing" in PE by a note from my parents. I can still remember that note I carried around all the time. I can remember it wet with sweat from my hip pocket and stained blue from new blue jeans. I remember peeling the note open for the substitute teacher and feeling dumb for it, but feeling safe and isolated at the same time.

Standing against the gym wall and watching everybody else dance, I must have had the conversation a hundred times:

"How come you're not dancing?"

"It's against my religion."

"What religion are you?"

"Protestant."

"I'm a Protestant," someone would always say quizzically. Of course when they said "Protestant" they meant anything that wasn't Catholic or Jewish. When I said "Protestant," I meant fundamentalist, Bible-toting, Scripture-quoting, sin-hating, nondancing, born-again believer with a note.

It was nice to have an excuse for not doing what intimidated me. In retrospect, I wonder how long I've excused myself from social endeavors in general, not just dancing. Excused from fun. Excused from friends. Excused from danger. Excused from conflict. Excused from love. Excused from life. Whatever it is, I've got a note here, excusing me. I think I sometimes act as though that blue jean–stained note from grammar school is still in my pocket; I've reached for it many times since.

Nursing a coffee drink alone is a little like having a note excusing me from participating, unless, of course, I want to. It says I'm busy. I'm doing something here. It's handy security for my isolation.

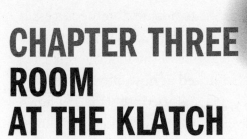

CHAPTER THREE
ROOM
AT THE KLATCH

There are three gourmet-coffee bistros within walking distance of my house. My favorite has the ideal setup for spending a couple of hours writing in the morning—an outdoor patio with an electrical outlet for my laptop. The patio has just enough road noise to garble most ambient conversation. Also, the bistro bakery serves a scrumptious coconut-butterscotch-oatmeal cookie that I order religiously along with a latte—my favorite coffee drink after too much early morning black coffee has brought the acid content in my stomach above tolerance level.

I have found that working in a public place helps stimulate my thinking and keep me alert. I'm less apt to stare off. As added inspiration, this bistro takes its name from coffeehouses in Shakespeare's London, where artists and intellectuals gathered in what were called coffee "klatches." Here they use *K* for both words: "The Koffee Klatch—Specialty Coffee, Food, and Desserts."

This place is as energizing as the caffeine it presses through its espresso machines. Inside, Internet access is available at four tables, two dollars for twenty minutes or five dollars an hour. It was one of the first Internet cafes in our area, and I am surprised at how often those Internet-access services are still used, considering how many people now have their own PCs. The only things stuffy about the atmosphere are two overstuffed chairs and a couch that blend in nicely with bistro tables and chairs.

The plum-colored walls double as a gallery, featuring the works of local artists. On the wall next to the counter is a little blurb about the artist on display and usually a personalized description of his or her work. The current exhibit comes from an international photographer who has captured colorful portraits of the common folk of India, China, and Nepal. She writes of her work: "While on a recent solo trip around the world, I discovered the profound art of communication without language. I found that photography was a wonderful way for me to connect with the various individuals that I met during my journey. Something incredible happens when you stop and truly allow yourself to consciously occupy a stranger's space. Whether invited by a glance or a simple gesture, somehow those few seconds of shared space would magically evolve into friendships, cups of tea, and unforgettable memories."

This quote could easily have been written about the experience of being in a gourmet coffee shop—right down to the tea and the memories. You consciously occupy a stranger's space, relishing your privacy while remaining open to the possibility that a glance or gesture might lead to a relationship (though it rarely does). It is a place where you can discover the profound art of communication without language.

Here is a truth about these trendy coffee shops that are now commonplace on America's suburban and upscale urban landscape: You walk into this place to stay for a while, and even if you can't stay, you tell yourself that one day you're going to bring a good book, sit in one of those comfortable chairs with a steaming brew, and forget the world. You tell yourself that, and it's almost as if you've done it, even when you haven't. In fact, to walk into one of these places is to have that experience in your mind, whether or not you have actually done it.

The service at the Koffee Klatch is warm and friendly. If I'm caught without cash, I make it up the next time. If I come to write and start right in because the line is too long, someone will often bring my regular latte out to me as soon as the rush lightens up.

Some days the line between server and clientele is blurred. On unusually busy days, I've seen the guy behind me in line jump over the counter and ask me what I wanted. Was he an off-duty server or someone so familiar with the procedure that he could do it himself? Either way, no one appears to mind. All of the servers sit down with customers and enjoy food or drink with them at one time or another. Those who work here often come in on their days off, because this klatch is really more than a coffeehouse; it's a community. And if you stay long enough, you discover it is a particular type of community—a gay community, to be exact.

I wasn't aware of it immediately. I didn't notice the magazines out on the patio right away. It wasn't until I observed some hugging over the counter that I began to get the point. The bond that exists here between staff and regular clientele presented a dilemma to me.

Do I stay or should I go? Is there an oppressive spirit here? Is it okay to use the bathroom? Is there something contagious on the tables? Did they put something in the cookies? Will I get HIV from touching anything? Even though I know better than to think seriously about any of these things, they still come to mind. The truth of the matter is: I'm uncomfortable here.

I wince when I face up to this discomfort. My stereotypical thinking must be painful for someone on the receiving end. I'm reminded of that great line from *Blazing Saddles* after Bart (played by Cleavon Little) holds himself ransom in front of the townspeople and, at gunpoint, forces himself inside the jailhouse. Bart sits down behind the desk, shakes his head, and says, "White people are so-o-o dumb." I just confirmed what many homosexual men must think all straight men think. And they're right.

My first known encounter with a homosexual man was a very difficult one. I was in my final year at Wheaton College, thirty miles from Chicago. I had signed with a religious record company for my first album, *The Cold Cathedral*. Someone from the Chicago-based company invited me downtown to meet the arranger and check out the musicians from Chicago's Old Town School of Folk Music, as well as the studio where, immediately upon graduation, I would spend a couple of weeks recording. He suggested I stay overnight in order to fit everything in. Rather than booking an expensive hotel room for me, he offered to put me up in his apartment.

That night he made a few passes at me that I initially mistook as friendly gestures. I was completely naive to homosexual relationships. Then later in a folk club, he bragged about me so much he had me singing up on stage. I think I was the only one in the place who didn't know what was really going on. I was his new protégé, soon to become, well . . . I still didn't know. A number of times that evening I remember this man saying to me, "Don't worry, I would never hurt you." Now why would you tell someone you wouldn't hurt him unless some-where in your mind you were planning to? That's when I began to get a clue and pushed him away.

Two months later, while recording in Chicago, I found out that the producer on the project was also a gay man. I sat up most of one night listening to this man's story. Contrary to what he portrayed, he was not a happy person. Even after he started to go straight, he still had a lot of emotional baggage to deal with—stuff that was harder, in a way, because he wasn't self-medicating with sex. I became a sort of confidant, a friend. I liked him. He was honest. The first man was not.

I left Chicago for Los Angeles recognizing that just as it was wrong for me to think that all straight men make advances toward women, it was wrong of me to think that all homosexual men make inappropriate advances toward men.

✳ ✳ ✳

So I keep going to the Koffee Klatch even though I feel somewhat uncomfortable about it. It's no longer about the patio writing and the cookies. It's about the individuals there and my need to face this tangled-up mishmash of fear of contamination, judgment, and my "better than thou" attitude. I want to know where and how God steps in with His love and grace, and how He handles the truth about His own ways and means.

Our neighbor is gay. She was surprised that neither my wife nor I altered our behavior toward her after finding this out about her. In fact, we are very happy we know her. Whether we are believers or in the process of seeking the face of God, we are all in pursuit of God's mercy.

God is the Creator and Designer of the human spirit,

and as such, He understands us and has created us in a uniquely complex and profound way. But He also created us with very narrowly defined needs. We all have a need to be known, and we all have a need to know. We need to be known by God and by others. And we need to know God and know others.

Love God. Love our neighbor. This, I believe, defines the very essence of our soul. We have a need for affirmation—to know that we are accepted just as we are. We have a need for community—loving relationships within a group of like-minded people. And we have a need for accountability to one another. We need to know that we're not the center of the universe and that our choices affect not only ourselves, but others as well.

However, there is a weight and cost in loving others as Christ loves me. It is heavy on my heart as I write because I know that if all I do is admit my failings on paper, my confession hasn't really cost me anything.

I wonder: Am I just writing to say I am a little uncomfortable as an occasional observer within this community, or am I searching my mind for answers to give these men? Answers work fine in classrooms, but they get more difficult in coffee shops. Are these people looking to me for the answers or do they even know they are sinners, as I am?

What is my motive in wanting to offer answers? Is it to speed up their change so I don't have to be so freaked out around them or pull my child away when a gay individual approaches? Imagine how that person must feel. And I am a little uncomfortable?

✳ ✳ ✳

"Would you be interested in an espresso I just made?" A new girl who worked at the Klatch was suddenly standing next to me, and I realized she was addressing me.

"Sure. Thank you very much."

It was her first day on the job, and she confessed to having made a mistake on an order. She had short, choppy hair streaked with turquoise and a good deal of metal piercing her face.

When I had placed my order earlier, she had undercharged me by a dollar at the counter. I knew she did because I always order the same thing. She let it go because she didn't know how to reopen the register. That's when she told me she was still learning the prices. So I put the difference between what she charged me and what it should have cost me, along with an appropriate tip, into the jar next to the register.

"Wide-awake now?" the turquoise-haired girl asked as she passed by a little later.

"Yep," I said, "wide-awake, thanks to you."

I know I am prone to judge, and that is one of the reasons why I come here (that and the cookies). I want to get over that propensity. I want to stop putting others down for anything, regardless of who they are and what flavor their sin is. Believe me, this is hard, because I've spent most of my life focusing on what makes *my* sin less of an abomination to God than someone else's.

Here at the Klatch, it's like a small town, and I realize that most everyone here is "out of the closet." They are who they are and they find community in their need. Me? I tend to be a closet sinner, keeping my coffee and my conversation to myself. So I keep coming back to the Koffee Klatch. And each time, I find my heart a little softer, a little more aware of how special everyone is in God's eyes.

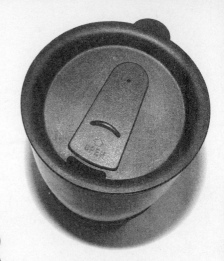

CHAPTER FOUR
FRANCES IN
PARADISE

It seemed perfectly natural when, shortly after my mother died, my dad decided to get in touch with Frances, the doctor's wife. As the remaining survivors of the quartet, it made perfect sense for my dad and Frances to turn to one another for comfort and companionship.

Dad even went up to see her in her home in Paradise, a small rural town in northern California. I have a feeling that he would have brought her back with him if she had been willing to leave. But she has her boys nearby, and she likes her life away from the city; and my dad has his church and his life in southern California. I don't know if the option of relocating up north was something he considered, but if it were me, I would have gone to be with Frances in Paradise in a heartbeat.

The Frances in my memory is as sweet as they come. She has smooth olive skin that never seemed to wrinkle, even with age. Petite, with a perfect oval face and dark eyes, she wore her dark hair in a bun pinned to the back of her head. I never saw her hair down but I surmised there was lots of it. She has no Native American blood, but I always pictured her as a squaw in buckskin, probably because of her dark skin and slight frame.

There always seemed to be a smile on her face. I cannot imagine her without that smile. It wasn't a big smile or a fake one. Just a quiet, sweet, Mona Lisa smile that never went away no matter what the circumstances. I don't remember her speaking much either—just smiling as I imagine a squaw would do, hearing everything but keeping quiet about most of it.

In relation to the interplay of surface impression and inner character, she and Hugh, her husband, were exact opposites. He was gruff, with a hide like an alligator, though inside was a soft spot of compassion that may explain why he was a doctor. Frances was always frail and delicate, but she possessed the inner strength of two people. She had to be this way to raise five boys. She is the closest thing I know to a steel magnolia.

I don't get it. My dad has already made the biggest move of his life: He sold the house I was born and raised in—the house he lived in for almost sixty years—and moved to Pasadena into an assisted-living one-bedroom apartment with a small deck facing the mountains. He can receive two prepared meals a day. Going through this transition almost crushed him. Now he's surrounded by strangers waiting out the end of their life.

How can that be better than Frances in Paradise? What's one more move when you've already left so much? Anyway, this move would bring warmth, friendship, companionship, and, yes, love.

I am no expert on what marriage is like at ninety, but my guess is that, more than anything, it is about companionship. At ninety, I don't think you get married for sex (though I wouldn't mind being wrong about this). You get married so as not to be alone. It's been that way from the beginning—even God agrees that being alone isn't a good idea. I don't think the need for companionship changes at ninety. My guess is that it becomes even more intense.

I'm pulling for this relationship, probably because I realize my own preference to be alone comes from something passed down from my father. His life always seemed so predictable. So safe. So much of it was lived in his favorite reclining chair. I imagine him in his apartment now and wonder what he does. There is a strain in me—some twisted part of my DNA—so bent on solitude that it would look favorably upon the total isolation that some predict will be the fate of those in hell. I fight that tendency all the time, and somehow it seems that my father abandoning his isolation for Frances in Paradise would be a small blow to its power over me.

I'm way too much alone, inside myself, at a time in my life when my relationships require the most of me. When I think of Jesus throwing Himself constantly into the lives of those around Him—telling us to be attached to our neighbor as much as we are to ourselves—I know this cannot be right. Nor do I get to blame anyone. We all find things in ourselves that we see magnified in our parents. We try blaming them for these things, but we have made our own mistakes just fine without their help.

What I found out later gave me a glimmer of hope in my battle with detachment. I pressed my dad further about his feelings for Frances and discovered that he would, in fact, move to Paradise if Frances were more interested. Apparently she's the hang-up, not him. She doesn't feel God wants her to get married again. That was good news for my DNA, though not for my dad. Something about this seems very tragic. Why couldn't two people, who have shared so much, live out their last few days together? What fear would keep this from happening?

"So what are you going to do about it?" I asked him.

"Nothing," he said.

"You're not going to try and persuade her? Come on, Dad. Don't give up."

Indeed, don't give up for my sake, if anything. All I could hear when he said this was "the Nothing"—that well-named evil force in the children's film classic *The NeverEnding Story*, which slowly eroded away all life, color, and imagination. The Nothing is my greatest adversary. It's not Satan or evil or temptation or even lust. It's the Nothing. It's the god of isolation that encourages being comfortable through noninvolvement—the false peace disguised as passivity. It's what can make you stare at a mountain for days without a thought in your head, and like it.

"So that's it? You'll never see her again?"

"I still call her once in a while, and I hope she'll still welcome a visit or two."

"That's not good enough," I wanted to say, but instead I said, "Don't give up. She may just be saying that part about God not wanting her to marry again because she's afraid or something."

This shouldn't be too hard. All I have to do is get God to change His mind and let Frances know about it. Of course, maybe she's just using God as an excuse for other reasons why she doesn't want to marry again or marry my dad in particular. Nevertheless, I take it as good news: He'd go if she said yes. That will have to do for now.

For his ninetieth birthday, my brother and sister and I got together and gave him a high-powered telescope on a tripod. From his deck, he can pick out people hiking in the San Gabriel Mountains, and, according to the claims on the box, he should be able to see Saturn's rings on a clear night. I bet from the roof of his twelve-story building, with his telescope trained properly, he can see all the way to Paradise.

CHAPTER FIVE
STARBUCKS
AND JESUS

A cartoon that ran in the *New Yorker* magazine shows a man and woman sitting in an intimate café surrounded by small bistro tables and chairs. A couch nestles in the corner, and at every table sculptured lamps reach down like fingers from the ceiling. Over large cups of steaming liquid, the man says to the woman, "Are we in this Starbucks or the one down the street?"[2]

Writers and connoisseurs of good coffee take a lot of swings at Starbucks these days, but that's only because it's easy to hit a big target. The mermaid in the middle of that famous green circle, the company's logo, makes a good bull's-eye. In Seattle, the word on the street is that countless little guys make better-quality coffee. I, for one, am amazed that Starbucks, in spite of its rapid and phenomenal growth, has maintained the level of quality it has championed for over twenty-five years—right down to its ground French Roast that I buy in the supermarket.

I discovered Starbucks before it was famous, which makes me even more loyal. I feel like immediate family. I found Starbucks coffee in 1978 when it was served in the cafeteria of Seattle Pacific College (now Seattle Pacific University). My whole understanding of coffee was revolutionized. It became something I actually liked—something more than an acquired taste or a necessary morning caffeine fix.

If it isn't obvious yet, I am a loyal, shameless consumer of the Starbucks brand. I drink my coffee every day out of a stainless-steel mug with a snap-on lid that I got at Starbucks three years ago. I have a Starbucks cap. I fly United whenever possible because the airline has a good frequent-flier program—and the fact that Starbucks is served on board does not go unnoticed. This Christmas, I bought my son a vintage red toy truck with the familiar green logo on the door panel and a Christmas tree in the truck bed. For myself, I bought a miniature porcelain mug ornament to hang on my own Christmas tree. I get a warm feeling inside when I'm on the road and I see its familiar logo. It's home away from home. I'm a deeply loyal, model customer. As far as I'm concerned, there is coffee and there is Starbucks, and that's about it. Coffee is what you get at Circle K or 7-Eleven. Starbucks is what you go a little out of the way for. Lest I lose some readers at this point, let me add that I know that Starbucks is not necessarily first on every coffee lover's list of great coffees. I have run into my share of anti-Starbucks sentiment, both from those whose taste tells them there are other, smaller brands that are superior, as well as from those who have a bone to pick with Starbucks' corporate success. This latter animosity has even led to vandalism of some franchises by those who are against the rise of global corporate megapowers. I don't wish to discuss either of these matters at this time; I merely refer to Starbucks as exemplary of a new style of bringing coffee to the marketplace. Its freshly roasted high-quality beans are a welcome option to the dry brown grind we used to buy in a big can with the roll-top can-opener key that we had to pry off the bottom. This same can later served as a spare paint can on everybody's worktable. That's how names like Maxwell House and Folgers used to show up regularly in everyone's garage.

When I say Starbucks, I also am alluding to all the coffee companies like Peet's Coffee, Seattle's Best, Tully's, Caribou, Pura Vida, and hundreds of other local blends that roast their own coffee and pack it, beans or ground, in a sealed, airtight brick-shaped package. We have a small coffee company here in my own town—Laguna Coffee Company—that has its own stainless-steel roaster in the middle of the store.

Even though these smaller brands are good quality, I can't always get them like I can get Starbucks (I can't get Laguna Coffee Company coffee in the Denver airport, for instance), so I stick with what I know. I go for reliability and availability. I am glad that Starbucks is a megacorporation, because that means I can find a decent cup of coffee pretty much everywhere I go.

Besides, I am a creature of habit. I'm the type who will order the same thing over and over again at my favorite restaurant so I don't end up wasting my money on something I won't like as much. And I have tried some of those other coffee brands, even ones that are chic in Seattle, and I've not been as happy as I would have been sticking to what I know.

My attempt to explain my loyalty to Starbucks is designed to lead to the next point in my thesis—that just about everything I can think of about my experience with Starbucks coffee also corresponds to something true about my experience with Jesus.

I'm loyal to Jesus because I feel that I found Him (or in this case He found me) before a lot of other people in my generation did. I was following Jesus before moral was a majority and Christian was a coalition. I was following Jesus when the Beatles were more popular than He was. I was following Jesus before the Jesus movement. And my commitment to Him continues in spite of a fast-growing, popularized Christian culture that makes my head swim with its array of products and services.

Just as there is coffee and there is Starbucks, I believe

that there is religion and then there is Jesus. I was very happy to find this out, because for me Christianity used to be an acquired taste. I grew up with it—even knew in my heart it was true—but that didn't mean I *liked* it. Meeting Jesus made me fall in love with God. I'm not into Jesus because I'm supposed to be, or because I grew up with Him, or because believing is a fire escape from hell. I'm into Jesus because I'm way over the top with Him. I love following Christ. I love the life I have with God. I love the world the way He shows it to me. I would follow Him no matter what.

My praising one brand of coffee over another doesn't mean I think it's the only quality coffee out there; like-wise I'm not saying my own experience of Jesus is the only legitimate one. I am merely saying that my Starbucks experience most closely captures my own personal experience with God.

I keep coming back to Starbucks because of the expe-rience I have there. The company made a promise to me—it promised me the world's best coffee delivered in a clean environment that always invites me to stop and stay awhile—and so far it has kept it. God has kept His promises to me as well, saturating the most difficult times in my life with His peace. I keep coming back to Him because of the wholeness I have in Him. I stick with my coffee for the same reason I stick with God. He completes me. Why would I look elsewhere? This is not just about habit; it is about being whole. It's about trust. It's about making and keeping promises.

Of course, like all of us, Starbucks is fallible. God always keeps His promises, but Starbucks has been known to break a few. Given my overwhelming level of satisfaction, I can weather this.

Once in an airport Starbucks, the person behind the counter was rude, disinterested, and actually lied to me—saying certain services were shut down when I knew they weren't. She just didn't want to put forth the effort to serve me. It was such a contrast to the usual, cheery, "I'm here to do anything I can to improve your coffee experience" attitude I usually encounter in a Starbucks that it stuck in my mind.

The only part of the coffee experience that doesn't translate to my faith experience in a positive way has nothing to do with a brand; it is the whole idea of decaffeinated coffee. Now I understand the reasons why decaffeinated coffee was developed and why any serious coffee company has to offer it in order to meet its customers' needs. I simply don't accept decaffeinated coffee as a general principle. Why would I drink coffee without caffeine?

Caffeine is the heart and soul of coffee. Without it, you just have taste, and although that taste can be acquired, you initially acquire a taste for coffee *because* of the caffeine. I can't imagine anyone drinking decaf from the get-go. It's a substitute for the real thing. It's for someone who has already become a coffee drinker, but for whatever reason can't have or doesn't want the caffeine. In my book, decaf is just not coffee. It's coffee without a kick.

I could describe my church experience for a long time as religion without a kick. I had a faith without the buzz—a sanitized human experience with its heart and soul removed. Don't misunderstand me. When I say heart and soul, I do not mean the Holy Spirit. I mean the guts of the human connection. Caffeine is a stimulant, and as a caffeinated Christian, I have come to realize that I need help on more than just a spiritual level.

I am a caffeinated Christian—a human being who bleeds and hurts and struggles and wants to run away from life sometimes. That's when I need a strong cup of java with a kick in it to propel me into the reality of my daily experience. My faith is a part of all this. Being a believer doesn't mean I cease being dysfunctional. I've got my Bible and a strong cup of coffee, and I need them both to make it today.

As I said before, my early experiences in the church could be described as a sort of decaffeinated Christianity—spirituality with the human element removed. We had church socials and prom night (without the dancing), we played Rook cards (regular cards were sinful, like gambling), and we watched Billy Graham movies. All of these things, like decaffeinated coffee, were substitutes for what people outside the church were doing. By creating our own version of these things, we showed that we really did have a taste for the world. We simply tried to take out what we thought was bad and still have the experience. Even Starbucks makes decaffeinated coffee, but that's only a concession for those who want the experience but for some reason can't have the caffeine. It's never the preferred drink. It's a substitute.

I have since come to understand that to decaffeinate my faith experience is to miss why Christ came into the world in the first place. He came to affirm my humanity and meet me in it—to meet me in Starbucks, as it were, not just in church. I have found that a realistic faith is a lot like regular coffee: it comes full strength and includes the bad parts along with the good. I can choose to be empowered by this kind of earthy faith, or I can choose a decaffeinated spirituality with the offensive parts taken out (or at least denied)—a life lived in a kind of sanitized bubble.

My caffeinated Christianity is a relationship with God that takes into account my life in this body and my handicap as a sinner. It's my need for a wake-me-up in the morning that does not exclude the Spirit's presence in my life. It's my way of connecting meaningfully with others. It's a holy connection with a human kick—an experience with Christ that would have held up quite well with my dancing classmates, had I given it a chance and not isolated myself.

Caffeine is what gets my blood pumping. I am aware of all the negative side effects—it shrinks my capillaries, it's addictive, it gives me acid stomach, it may shorten my life, and it will eventually kill me—but life isn't exactly kind to me either, and knowing that does not hinder my faith. Indeed, it makes faith more real. This is life as I know it in the world—the one I'm in, the one

God loves, and the one Jesus came to. It's the world full of people God is crazy about, even though many of them don't know it.

The thing about Starbucks is that it helps me celebrate this world, and I maintain my loyalty because it is the first brand of coffee that did this for me. I felt a little guilty about drinking coffee at first, just as for a long time I felt guilty about being human. Then I realized that being human was God's idea, and Jesus, His Son, is the very celebration of its essence. So order a dark brew of your favorite brand of coffee, pull up a chair with me, and let's think about the ramifications of spirituality on caffeine.

CHAPTER SIX
PROFESSIONAL
CHRISTIAN

Hold it now. With any good thing there is a limit, and in my opinion if there is any undesirable practice in marketing to the American consumer, it is product over-kill. If something is successful, marketers inflict upon us as many varieties of that something as possible to take full advantage of its success. Today, for instance, we do not just have a successful movie; we have merchandise to go along with the movie, product placement of the merchandise in the movie, and corporate tie-ins with other products that enhance its exposure.

My commitment to Starbucks takes into account the coffee, the service, and the atmosphere. I do not go to

Starbucks to order a double-vanilla, half-decaf mocha-chino with extra foam. In fact in all the years I have supported Starbucks, I have never ordered anything other than coffee or a latte (not including scones, cookies, chocolate muffins, or pound cake—which I admittedly have consumed too much of for my own good). In other words, I'm into Starbucks for the quality coffee, not all the foofy drinks.

This product overkill has affected every aspect of the market, even the sale of Bibles. Purchasing a Bible these days is a little like ordering a cup of coffee at a Starbucks. King James? New King James? Revised Standard? New International? Today's New International? *New American Standard?* New Living Translation? *The Message?*

I can understand how someone in the market for a Bible could walk out of a bookstore without one.

Here's how to get a blank stare from a clerk in a bookstore. Say: "I just want to buy a Bible. Can someone please sell me a Bible?" Order a cup of coffee in Starbucks and you might get a similar reaction. At the very least, the clerk will want to know if you want regular or decaf. Tall, venti, or grande? Dark or medium roast?

All these choices make us connoisseurs, whether we like it or not. It seems to me we are becoming connoisseurs of more things every year. Who would have thought, thirty years ago, that people would pay good money for a plastic bottle full of what you used to get out of the tap. Aquafina, Arrowhead, Crystal Springs, Evian, and Perrier—everyone's an expert on which brand is best. This is water we're talking about—one of the basic elements of life.

We have become professional coffee drinkers. We know the subtleties and nuances of all the options. I've noticed something about this. Once you become a professional, you can't go back to being a novice. You can't fake inexperience. You can't talk yourself into something less than what you know. I drank tap water for years and never gave it a second thought. But now that I have tasted the pure sweetness of bottled water, I have to admit that the chlorinated stuff tastes awful. You can't go back to being naive once you've had your eyes opened. You can't tell yourself you don't know what a good cup of coffee is once you've had one. Sometimes I think I would have been better off not knowing. Just now, for instance, I spent twenty-five minutes locating a Starbucks because the coffee at the hotel where I am currently staying left so much to be desired.

I wonder if the same principle is at work in matters of faith. I wonder if you can become a professional Christian and lose something plain and simple in the process. And if you do, can you go back?

When I first met my wife, Marti, she was not a professional Christian. She didn't know one Bible translation from another, and it didn't matter. She could open any Bible to any place and find something meaningful for herself and for those around her.

✳ ✳ ✳

Marti met Christ through a rather bizarre series of events that included dating the wayward son of a Baptist pastor. It was 1970, and she was a "stewardess" in an era when it was still okay to use that term. The job still retained a little of its "coffee, tea, or me" glamour. Long fake lashes and sculptured hairstyles were part of the standard uniform of the day.

Marti met the minister's son when her roommates—all stewardesses—snagged him on a return flight to their Los Angeles domicile and, on a dare, brought him home to meet her. He was wayward enough to go along with the caper. A relationship ensued, and in the process, Marti became acquainted with the man's library. As she says, "Had they been books on baseball, I would have studied baseball." But they were books on God and Christianity, and unlike this young man, they remained faithful to their message—a message of God's mercy that finally reached Marti one night as she was alone in her bed. She had an unforgettable experience with Christ, who touched her with His love and flooded her with His mercy. No one administered this to her. It was just Marti and God.

This was a turn of events the pastor's son had not anticipated. Spiritually, Marti leapfrogged over him and sought out his father in her search for the answers to her myriad of questions.

On her first visit to his office, Marti bypassed the

church secretary and barged right in unannounced. The pastor received her graciously in spite of it. She put her feet up on his desk, and smoke from her cigarette filled the room as he searched for a makeshift ashtray. Marti was totally unaware that smoking was nearly a mortal sin in a Baptist church. To this day she is embarrassed over how rude she was, but the pastor never blinked. He actually seemed to take joy in her eager, genuine heart and uninformed irreverence.

"How can I trust that what you say is the truth?" she asked.

"You can't," he told her. "You have to find out for yourself."

"What do I need to do?"

At that the pastor began a minicourse of Bible interpretation. Like a doctor giving a prescription, he sent her out with a list of tools to purchase: A *New American Standard Bible*, *Strong's Exhaustive Concordance*, and *Vine's Expository Dictionary of New Testament Words*. When the pastor mentioned that many words in Greek and Hebrew often translate to only one word in English and to recapture the more subtle meanings you have to know something about the original languages, Marti insisted on knowing how to do that. That's what the books were all about. He also got an associate on the phone and registered her in a seminary-level school.

But Marti didn't wait for school to become an ardent recruiter for God. She jumped right in. Before each flight, she prayed for two specific people: someone she could

introduce to the Lord and someone who already knew
Him who would encourage her. She purposely chose the
shortest flight segments so she could get in as many as five
flights a day.

It was her method of doing this that broke all molds.
She took all her newly prescribed Bible-study books on
board (we're talking more pages than a pilot's flight
manual) and would strike up a conversation with a
passenger. As soon as Marti identified some problem or
dilemma in that person's life that could be captured in a
word, she would look that word up in her concordance
and find related Scriptures. Working together, she and
her passenger would dig through the Scriptures together
until they found an answer.

"Is there anything here you don't understand?" she
would ask. "Well, let's look it up." This was a little like
you or me going out on the golf course with Tiger
Woods' clubs, having barely a clue as to what to do with
them. No matter. She wasn't a professional Christian.
She was a spiritual midwife in midair in a uniform.

"Would this be a good opportunity for you to accept
the Lord?" she would ask.

"I don't know," was often the honest response.

"Well, I know for myself that if you believe in your
heart that the Lord is the Son of God and confess with
your mouth that He is Lord, you're in." (This was Marti's
version of Romans 10:9, which she didn't get quite right,
but that didn't seem to matter too much.)

"I can do that."

"Good. Let's pray. You start."

"Do I have to close my eyes?"

"We're above the clouds. . . . I don't think God will mind either way."

Marti couldn't help it. Her joy was welling up inside. She was overwhelmed by God's forgiveness. The fact that the free gift of salvation was offered to all people meant that everyone simply had to know about this. You couldn't have stopped her from doing this any more than you could stop a runaway train.

What Marti didn't know was her greatest asset. She didn't know the "right" way to share her faith. Her limited understanding of the Bible and her unorthodox use of Bible-reference tools only proved how much she wanted to share her joy with people. I know God smiled on all of this and was able to do His work quite well, thank you.

It's because of this nonprofessional aspect of her Christianity that Marti has been, from the beginning of our relationship until now, the best thing that has happened to me aside from knowing Christ. Even when she heard me perform my music in those early days, she could never figure out why people applauded. Not that it wasn't great, but it was just John. She's never seen "special" as being anything special. Why get all worked up over a good cup of coffee?

Marti simply has never been a professional Christian. She is oblivious to the rules of professionalism; she just likes being around people who want to be free. When everyone's trying to meet someone else's standard, it's easy to lose the joy of being free. I think this was the reason the pastor didn't mind her audaciousness in his office: He realized he had been around Christians so long, he had lost the whole point of his message. Marti's unprofessional faith reminded him of the joy of his own salvation.

I am learning this, too, through a painful process of facing the addiction to self-righteousness and judgment that goes along with being a professional Christian. I know what it is to get professional about my sin: It means to hide it. Professional Christianity means I have a reputation to maintain at all cost, even if that leads to dishonesty. Sometimes I wish I could go back to being an amateur, but I'm too experienced for that. I have to press on to find my professional sin. I have hidden it so well for so long that I have to search to discover where I put it.

For the longest time, I equated being a Christian with being good. That meant as a Christian leader, I not only had to be good, I had to be better. Now I realize that being good is the least important thing about being a Christian. In fact, I'm a Christian because I know I'm *not* good. I'm a Christian because I found out the fantastic news that God loves me anyway. Of course, my wife has known this all along.

CHAPTER SEVEN
INVOLUNTARY
DETOX

I once lectured for three days at a college in Nebraska that is affiliated with a group of churches that treat caffeine as a drug on par with nicotine, alcohol, and marijuana. These churches also hold their weekly church services only on Saturday. Even though they are Christians, they like to continue the Jewish tradition of Sabbat, or seventh day—the day God rested from six days of Creation. In spite of these rather legalistic traditions, I found the students, teachers, and administrators at this school to be some of the nicest people I have ever been with.

As is often the case at schools like this, they put me up in guest housing on campus, and I ate all my meals in the dining hall. This is one of the few drawbacks to this odd career I have chosen. As a frequent speaker at colleges and universities across the country, I am often subjected to dining-hall food, something for which there should definitely be a maximum sentence of only four years.

I've learned a few tricks about managing the dining hall as an adult, however. I ask the students to tip me off on what to look for and what to avoid. I look for the longer lines (which lead to the more popular items). And if a large number of students seem to be having Fruit Loops for dinner, I take that as a sign to stay away from everything. The savior of college dining-hall food for some time has been the cereal station and the salad bar, though even the latter sometimes can present problems. If the mushrooms are out of a can, the hard-boiled eggs have been sliced off a roll like salami, and the bacon bits are imitation, you may end up with lettuce and ranch dressing. Still, it beats corn dogs or everything-left-over-from-last-night casserole.

On the second day of my visit, I began to get a headache that would not go away. This is very rare for me. I hardly ever get headaches unless I'm sick. But I wasn't sick; I felt fine otherwise. By the morning of the third day, I was having trouble concentrating. The pain was incessant, and on top of that I felt sluggish, as if I didn't have all cylinders firing. That, too, was unusual because I am used to being alert and quite stimulated while on the road—alert to people and challenged by students and lively discussion. I started asking if perhaps there was a headache virus going around, but no one knew anything about that.

At lunch on the third day, I went back for a second cup of coffee, hoping maybe a little extra caffeine would get me going. For the first time, I noticed that the top of the coffeepot was green plastic. I hadn't seen that before, and associating green with decaf, I asked one of the servers if it was decaffeinated coffee.

He looked at me as if I were asking if the University of Nebraska had a football team and said, "All our coffee is decaffeinated."

"You don't have any regular coffee?"

"Nope. You won't find any caffeine on this campus anywhere—even in the Coke machines. We're completely caffeine-free."

There was my problem. I'd been in involuntary detox for three days. At my first opportunity I snuck across the street to the gas-station convenience store and cased the joint for the expected burner-baked, carcinogen-laced rotgut brew that was probably in its third hour in the bottom of a round glass pot.

I debated finding a better brew (in a university town I knew there were bound to be gourmet coffee shops), but I had no time for that. I just needed to get the drug in my system and get back to campus.

I was surprised at how wicked I felt doing this. You

would have thought I snuck out of drug rehab to hit up the first dealer I could find. The guy behind the counter was foreign and didn't speak very good English. I could swear he gave me an evil eye as I paid for my coffee. Random people in the minimart cast sinister glances my way. And as I walked out the door with my steaming "Big Gulp" full of liquid headache relief, it seemed as if all eyes were on me. I felt as if the whole campus was aware of what I was doing—like an alarm had sounded as soon as I came out the door with my hot coffee in hand. I wondered if the college caffeine police would be waiting for me as soon as I crossed the street.

My wife has told me numerous stories of single moms avoiding the church because they felt they were being judged. I think I can understand a little how that feels now. It makes little difference whether you actually are being judged or if you simply feel as if you are. The fear of being judged is a real feeling, and it is usually a factor in creating the distance between people, especially in social status and lifestyle. I heard of one such mom who made it to church on three separate occasions but could not get any farther than the parking lot. She just couldn't bring herself to go in. Apparently the third time, a woman at the church thought she was lost and went to see if she could help. That broke the ice. When the church member found out what was happening, she wisely took the visitor and her kids out for coffee where they could first establish a relationship so church would not be so intimidating.

It didn't matter if the judgment the single mom feared was real or not. The feeling was real to her. The way to overcome these fears is to downplay the differences between people and emphasize similarities. The coffee shop was the perfect place to do this. By meeting over coffee, the woman from the church was able to bring out the similarities in a relationship.

Judging always creates distance. I think that may be why I judge. I want to keep a distance and accentuate differences with people or groups I don't like. When I'm close to someone and see how much I am like that person, it's hard to judge him or her.

Meanwhile, I returned to campus a little wiser with my caffeinated coffee in hand. I knew that I needed to be more aware of what my distance creates in people, and I needed to be willing to bridge that gap. In the future, instead of bringing others right into a threatening environment, perhaps it would be wise to take them out for coffee a few times first—as long as it is for real coffee. Stay away from that decaffeinated stuff unless you know what you're doing.

CHAPTER EIGHT
TROUBLE WITH
REGULAR

Soon after moving my family to Massachusetts in 1983, I noticed something odd about ordering coffee in New England. Every time I did, the waitress would ask me if I wanted it "regular." I would say yes, thinking she meant regular as opposed to decaf. When my coffee came, I would stare at the cream-colored liquid in my cup and say, "Excuse me, but I didn't ask for cream in my coffee."

"You said regular."

"Yes, but that's not what I was talking about. I assume this is regular. . . ."

"Well then, what seems to be the problem?"

Argghhh.

This happened a number of times until I finally understood that in Massachusetts, *regular* doesn't have anything to do with whether the coffee is caffeinated or not, it means coffee with cream and sugar already added. If you want caffeinated black coffee in Massachusetts, you don't want it regular. *Regular* has to do with coffee coming black or white. Whether it's caffeinated or decaf is another thing entirely.

So I finally got the regular thing down in relationship to life in New England, but in terms of life in general, I must confess, I'm still having trouble with regular.

* * *

You have no idea how hard it is to be famous when no one knows who you are. Throughout my life, I have accomplished things that usually would give a person a fair amount of notoriety. I am a recording artist, a published author, and a regular columnist in a national magazine. I have also been on radio and television and am in considerable demand as a speaker.

But when I meet people for the first time and they ask, "What do you do?" the question that follows my answer is inevitable: "Should I know you?" Of course what they actually mean is: "Are you *somebody*? Are you a celebrity? Would I recognize your name?" I never know exactly what to say in response to this. In a recent article in the *New Yorker*, a struggling movie actress commented on the same situation. "It's a trick question," she said. "If you say, 'Yes, as a matter of fact I am [somebody],' you are stuck-up. If you say no, then you're saying, 'I'm nobody special.'"

In my case, the reason no one recognizes me or knows my name is that most of my life has happened in an alternative sidebar to mainstream culture. I've been on Christian radio and television, my books and CDs are sold in Christian bookstores, I write for Christian magazines and speak to Christian audiences. Many people are not even aware this market exists. It's also no guarantee that the people who do know of this market have heard of me either, as I command a relatively small following even within this alternative culture.

This situation has created a huge discrepancy between my two personas. When I am on the road, by sheer nature of the invitation, I am going to a place where I am known as "somebody," at least to the extent that my ideas and presentations are worth paying me to come share them. It's easy in these environments to think, *Finally, I am in my element. The earth has solidified under my feet. The planets have come into alignment. Things are as they should be.*

Unfortunately, that experience doesn't last long. As soon as I arrive at the airport for the flight home, I revert to anonymity and return to a litany of relationships that are wanting, neglected loved ones, and an answering machine full of bill collectors vying for my attention who don't give a rip about who I am as long as they get a piece of what I'm bringing home. It's enough to make me want to get right back on a plane and fly back to where my name means something.

I would like to think that the people I meet on the road get the real me, but to be honest, the bill collectors probably get the guy that more closely resembles the truth. Bruce Cockburn has a song "The Trouble with Normal," and ever since I first heard the title I have thought of it as my theme song. I have a problem with normal—and by normal I mean being around people who don't know who I am other than *that guy who lives next door* or *the one who always buys groceries with that cute little kid* or *the one who comes in here all the time for a latte and a cookie.* These people don't know, or care, about my other persona. I would like to know what it is to be normal around the butcher, the baker, etc., but I always seem one size too large or too small for the fit. For me, "normal" seems to be something I can never be if I consciously aspire to be "someone," and I can't seem to kick that desire.

My wife tells a story about how she and a friend of hers—both of whom had been influential at a well-known resort—returned there recently and noticed how fast they had been forgotten. While standing in line at a popular restaurant—a restaurant where formerly they would have immediately been escorted to a table ahead of everybody—her friend exclaimed: "Doesn't anybody know who we *were*?" My sentiments exactly.

✳ ✳ ✳

An encyclopedia came to my door recently with my name in it. It was Randall Balmer's *Encyclopedia of Evan-*

gelicalism, in which I am listed between "Fire-Baptized Holiness Church of God of the Americas" and "Flannelgraph." Now this means something to me. This is important. There I am in black and white in an *encyclopedia*, no less. Everybody knows encyclopedias are a reliable source of unbiased knowledge and information.

That evening at an Anaheim Angels game with my four-year-old in tow, I reflected on the thirty-five thousand baseball fans in attendance and wondered how many of them could say their name was listed in an encyclopedia. But then I started imagining a special notice going up on the big screen: "Ladies and Gentlemen: Among our honored guests today, please welcome John Fischer, listed in the *Encyclopedia of Evangelicalism* as helping 'to spark a spiritual renewal coincident with the Jesus movement,'" and 34,998 people would probably say to themselves, "Huh?" The exception, of course, would be my son, to whom, at four years old, I am a really big deal for all the right reasons.

I'd like to think about this encyclopedia entry as a big deal, but I know it's not. Most people are important in a collection of some kind or another that only means something within that group, whether it's a church directory, a Rotary Club roster, or a family photo album. And anyway, being listed next to "Flannelgraph" should have been my first clue that being in this encyclopedia is a big deal only to a small circle of people who possibly might know what that is.

Doesn't anybody know who I *was*?

No, my trouble is with normal, and what is normal, if it isn't the people I regularly encounter in my day-to-day life? People such as neighbors, clerks, and other Starbucks customers. My trouble with normal is that I am nobody when I stand there in front of you with no prepaid publicity.

What makes me somebody doesn't mean much to most people, and without that head start, I have to start from scratch. If you don't already know who I am, and if I tell you and it still doesn't matter, then I feel helpless. I feel pretty naked out there. Maybe I should carry around a news clip and a brief bio.

Am I alone in this? Do you have a public and private persona—places where you are "somebody" and places where you are anonymous? Learning to bring these two into harmony is probably a good sign of mental health. As it is, my two personas appear to be so divergent I haven't even tried to reconcile them. I end up disconnecting either way. I am either somebody and aloof or nobody and inhibited. And if I sound like I'm making myself out to be a victim, it's only because that is a comfortable place to be, a place where no action is required.

Not long ago I had a very graphic representation of these extremes within a couple of hours. The first was the unique experience of sitting in on a study group of women, sixty-five and over, who act as a support team for an inner-city work among "gutterpunks"—homeless kids who live on the streets and in alleys of urban centers.

These grand ladies are a force to be reckoned with. It's an odd merger—punks and grandmas—but I am convinced there is no one who can love these kids better than they can.

"I don't want you to do a thing," the leader of the group had said (he was using one of my books as a catalyst for their study). "I just want you to sit and observe. I'll introduce you as a friend of mine who is visiting. I want you to experience firsthand what these women are getting out of your book. Some of them have been in this church all their life and they want to know why they haven't heard anything like this before. Trust me, you will be amazed." How could my ego resist?

In the thirty minutes of their study, every stereotype of grandmas I ever had was shattered. These ladies were sharp, witty, and took in new ideas like hungry wolves. They were animated and inquisitive. They were not afraid to be challenged in their thinking. My wife always called my mom "a wild woman waiting to happen." Well, I was in a room full of wild women *happening*.

When the teacher finally revealed my identity, a loud noise erupted in the room as they exclaimed their surprise and delight. But their comments to me afterward were most revealing: "I've been thinking these things for some time; it's good to find someone finally saying it."

"You articulated for me what I've been suspecting."

And the most telling of all: "You know, we've got to make some changes around here." And I knew that they would. These are not women used to sitting around exchanging pleasantries. These are people who care deeply about acting on God's will. And that day, they were like generals going over their battle plan. I came to hear some old ladies talk about my book and walked in on a strategy session for change.

Alas, and to my benefit, I realized their high view of me was not because I was a celebrity, but because they appreciated the contribution I'd made to their own growth and understanding. These women were taking what I wrote and acting on it. I had to stop and ask myself if I was doing the same. My wife often comments that something affects me long enough to write about it. Once I get it into words, it's as if I have it. But in actuality, I don't; I just wrote it down. I haven't really mastered anything until I've acted on it.

Two hours later I was downtown, face-to-face with a seventeen-year-old gutterpunk who had never read one of my books, didn't know who I was, and wouldn't care if she did, at least any more or less than she would care for anyone else. She had jet-black hair, dark makeup, and a spiked dog collar around her neck with a heavy chain hanging from it. Her black leather jacket looked inadequate to hold back the bitter November wind that was whipping through a canyon of skyscrapers. And did I mention she was holding a warm cup of Starbucks? I wondered, with all the metal piercing her lips, how she could drink hot coffee. She was two states away from her home and glad of it, because home meant sexual abuse at the hands of a stepfather and an uncle. It seemed fitting in light of her present transitory home that her name was Allie.

I am the father of a daughter, so to be near a homeless seventeen-year-old and not feel anything but uncomfortable reflected some kind of very serious disconnect on my part. Had I been able to find my heart in that moment, I would have hugged her to shield her from the cold, picked her up, and taken her home in my arms. None of those things even entered my mind. Instead I wanted to get away. It was no fault of hers. She gave me no reason to be inhibited. In fact, her sweetness defied an appearance that frightened me. She spoke freely to me and was even kind to my four-year-old son. The two of them exchanged ideas, but I could not find anywhere to connect. I had a hard time getting any words out.

I know now that shame made me disconnect with Allie, even for that brief encounter. I was ashamed for her predicament, and even though I did not actually contribute to it, I also didn't intend to do anything about it. Even though I knew that Allie might be heading for trouble, why couldn't I embrace her? I think I saw my daughter in Allie and recognized the ways in which I have failed her as well. As I stood with Allie, it was much easier to look away—to wait for this painful encounter to be over so I could move on to something else and forget about it.

Can I forgive myself and make restitution?

Of course, Allie had no clue about any of this. In fact, she was not asking anything from me. I was not going to resolve her problems in five minutes, yet I guarantee I could have done a lot more for her in those five minutes had I not been tied up inside myself. As it was, I called my daughter as soon as I could to find out how she was doing. I think I have Allie to thank for that.

✳ ✳ ✳

So what does any of this have to do with being "somebody" to eleven wild women and "nobody" to a seventeen-year-old gutterpunk? Mainly it is the fact that it doesn't matter how I feel either way. The truth of the matter is, *I* don't matter. Of course, I matter to God, just like you do, but in terms of those around me, I don't matter. If I could just get this, I might notice someone else for a change—maybe even put myself in his or her shoes. The real reason I felt like somebody around eleven women didn't have that much to do with me anyway; the reason I felt like nobody to Allie was because she was nobody to me. My little son was somebody to her and she didn't even know him.

There was a Starbucks across the street, and I noticed that as we slipped in there for coffees to go, I suddenly felt safe. My host had merely wanted me to see and experience some of the work they were doing in the inner city. He wanted me to meet some of the kids. I did and experienced so much more.

I've gone through most of my life with a secret. "Don't you know who I am?" Now I can answer that question myself: "Nobody of real interest, compared to you."

I think of myself now in the *Encyclopedia of Evangelicalism* in between "Fire-Baptized Holiness Church of God of the Americas" and "Flannelgraph," and I know that I would rather be appreciated by eleven grandmas and maybe someday by Allie or someone like her than listed in an encyclopedia. Most importantly, I want to be appreciated by my daughter.

CHAPTER NINE
THE END OF
WITNESSING

There is now a definite vocabulary for coffee drinkers. A coffee drinker's speech is likely to be laced with terms like cappuccino, latte, mocha, and espresso (if you are not well-informed you might call it *ex*-presso as I did before my spell-checker first flagged the error). If you happen to frequent Starbucks, you know that *tall, grande,* and *venti* are in-house lingo for the more ordinary *small, medium,* and *large.* Ordering coffee for the first time in a gourmet coffee bar is a little like being in Paris or Rome and trying to order in another language. One can feel quite intimidated.

It's not unusual for a group or product to develop its own inside language. For instance, in the airline industry you might hear about "an expected ETA of 0–nine hundred hours flying from O-R-D to L-A-X." Or there's the baseball announcer who describes players "shagging flies" before the game, "holding runners on," and "going to the rubber." If you're not on the inside, you simply don't understand what's going on.

In the same way, the community of people I grew up with had its own language. For instance, do you know what a "sword drill" is? What about "flannelgraph"? Do you know what it means to "backslide" or to be "luke-warm" or "on fire"? Does "winning souls" have anything to do with fast running shoes? What happens when you "go to the Lord"?

Often it's not necessarily a new term as much as it is a different interpretation of a common one. For instance, one of the key words for my youth group was *witness*. In common language, a witness is someone who testifies in court for either the prosecution or the defense. A witness is someone brought in by either side whose knowledge is relevant to the case. But in a strictly evangelical context, witness is something you do when you go out and find someone to tell about Christ, with the desired end of having that person accept Him as Savior. This task was drilled into me in Sunday school, so that I came to view the whole world as a mission field. Everyone I met was a potential convert who would perish without hope if I didn't witness to him or her. Of course, there was no guarantee that he or she would respond, but if I told someone about Jesus, then the blood was off my hands.

In the King James Version (the most commonly used translation when I was a child), the great commission found in Mark 16:15 says: "Go ye into all the world, and preach the gospel to every creature." As a child I took this to mean I should be preaching to anything that moved: dogs, cats, friends, and foes. "Every creature," it says. Based on my interpretation, I failed the great commission every day, except for my dog, who in the end was probably a believer anyway.

Now coffee can be a help or a hindrance to the propagation of the great commission. Certainly good conversation over coffee can lead to the opportunity for deeper insights, but coffee can also be a substitute for companionship. Personally, I have observed the world from behind too many cups of coffee, too afraid to come out. Now admittedly this is in direct violation of the great commission, but for me over the years, the pressure to witness to others has achieved the opposite of the desired effect.

All that compounded failure to preach to all the creatures I pass by day after day heaps up a mound of guilt that becomes more and more difficult to climb out of. It also clouds my relationships with those around me, making ordinary, natural friendships almost impossible.

In many ways, being a Christian in what is perceived to be a hostile world can be compared to being in a maximum-security prison by choice. "Lock me up," I say, holding out my hands for the obligatory handcuffs.

"I want the security of knowing no one can touch me in here." Happy to have all dangerous weapons confiscated, no conflicting worldviews, and only minimal contact with anyone outside, my willingness to give up freedom in exchange for safety is a pretty accurate description of the way these values stack up. I know about this. I've served my time. (It's actually quite common for some criminals who have served long prison terms not to want to leave even when they've been paroled. They have learned to manage in prison and the outside world is too scary for them.)

The only way a prison inmate can talk to someone on the outside is through a window of thick, bulletproof glass. He can talk with his visitors, but only by way of a phone line. This image characterizes much of my witnessing experience. Safe and protected in a controlled environment where I periodically encountered visitors for a limited time, I touched no one. We looked at each other through glass, but no closer than that. I even welcomed the guard's intrusion on the encounter, which meant I could return to the comfort and privacy of my own cell.

Then there are those times when fellow inmates joined me on work crews, all of us dressed in our orange jumpsuits and shackled together. I've done beach evangelism, street evangelism, airport evangelism, door-to-door evangelism, crusade evangelism, and inner-city evangelism. Our modus operandi was always the same: We bused in, did some digging and tilling of the soil, and we bused out. I always liked busing out the best.

Confession: As a Christian, I am the bearer of a message packed full of love for people I am afraid to be around.

Doesn't that sound rather convoluted? Stay away from the sinners but tell everybody about Jesus. How do you do that? Mixed messages like this have created a history of contradictions for Christians. On one hand I hold within me a loving message, overflowing with forgiveness and mercy and a new beginning for all. On the other, I'm uncomfortable being around people who don't believe what I believe. The contradiction is even built into the behavioral code: Witnessing to people you don't know is okay; hanging around them is not. It's got to be hit-and-run for your own safety.

Being "different" was highly prized in witnessing. This difference was created by a false view of self that took some well-devised cultural behavioral mechanisms to maintain. I learned to guard myself from what made me human lest I connect to the needs, wants, and failures in me that are common to everyone. We had to be different so we would stick out. Well, we stuck out all right, but we stuck out more like Nerds for Christ than anything else.

I can only guess what a truly unpleasant experience it must have been to encounter someone like me on one of those witnessing work crews. I never gave even the slightest consideration to those I talked to. I never asked about their interests. I was defensive from the start. I think I thrived more on being rejected than accepted. Being rejected was part of the motif. It was our persecution that ensured we were joining the martyrs. What if people had responded positively or hugged me? That would have gotten messy. The bottom line is clear: I wasn't there for them; I was there for myself. This was something I had to do to relieve all that pent-up guilt. The people we witnessed to were just a prop for our assignment. There was no relationship and no promise of one. It was the sort of setup that ensured I would always be witnessing to strangers.

In my childhood, a non-Christian friend would have been an oxymoron. We didn't have such a relationship. The "unchurched" were a part of a world full of enticements I might not be able to resist. So I witnessed to strangers but avoided them as friends. We bused in; we bused out.

I know that I love people, but this love is covered up with a good deal of embarrassment, fear, guilt, and self-righteousness. When I meet a non-Christian, all kinds of thoughts rush through my head: *I really wish I was better than you, but I'm fully aware that I am not. Getting too close to you can be a little like fraternizing with the enemy. When you are kind to me, I don't know what to do. You are messing everything up. I'm supposed to be happy as a Christian; you are supposed to be a sad and desperate sinner, so when you cheer me up with a smile or a friendly hello, it kind of takes the wind out of my spiel.*

There are two principles that have traditionally been labeled in Christianity as "greats." One is the great commission about sharing the good news of Christ's triumph over sin and death with every creature; the other is the great commandment, in which Jesus summed up all the law and prophets by telling us to love God and our neighbor as we love ourselves. Of these two, the commandment far outweighs the commission. I know what it is to carry out the commission without bothering with the command. We preached to strangers we didn't love and walked away feeling like martyrs, when all along we were just being obnoxious. To love someone, regardless of that person's religious affiliation, is to be vulnerable and open to the possibility that together we can come to know Christ's love and forgiveness in spite of ourselves. This is when both of these mandates get carried out in spite of us. Or think of it this way: One can carry out the commission without a thought for the commandment and end up losing an opportunity for both. But to carry out the commandment all but assures the commission will be carried out as well, since telling people about the love and forgiveness of God is a big part of loving them as we love ourselves.

Someone I know led a seminar for ministers in which he reminded them of the great commandment. He then asked them to write down the names of their neighbors on either side and across the street and to tell a little about each one of them. According to my friend, most of the ministers could only sit there with pen in hand and a blank sheet of paper in front of them.

I know my neighbors pretty well, but this has nothing to do with my conscious endeavor to love them—certainly nothing I can take any credit for, especially given my propensity to avoid them.

I live in a very tight, little community with eight dwellings bordering our property. It's pretty hard to avoid people here. It's hard to avoid the neighbor across the street who heard the last talk I gave on the subject of worry and who reminds me of my very words all the time now.

It's hard to avoid my neighbors with a wife like mine, who, when I was avoiding people on planes, was a flight attendant, chatting with all of them, introducing them to Christ—even bringing some who needed a home, home with her. And she's still inviting people over. She instigated a "welcome us" party when we first moved into this neighborhood and fifty people showed up. It's kind of hard to avoid people when you're married to Marti.

And it's hard to avoid your neighbors when your kids' evening activities keep them up at night and the adults end up inviting themselves over, preferring to join the party rather than fight the noise.

Yes, it's hard—even impossible—to avoid the people in our neighborhood. Even though I would prefer to be isolated, I live in a world that won't allow it. I've been pulled out of my prison into relationships with my neighbors and others outside my comfort zone who are altering the way I view people and the world around me.

That's why I've decided I'm not going to witness to people anymore, I'm just going to see if they want to join me for coffee. It's time to crawl out from behind this cup and find out what I have in common with all the other caffeine fanatics here. I have a feeling I might even learn some things about myself. It's time to get over myself and start being a friend. Isn't that what Jesus would do? If I could just get out of these handcuffs, I might find out.

CHAPTER TEN
ME AND THE AX
MURDERER

August was nearing and my daughter's birthday was less than two weeks away. For the last five summers, Anne has worked for U.S. Ocean Safety as a lifeguard up and down a ten-mile stretch of southern California's most popular beaches. She talked often about getting her fellow lifeguards all together before the summer was over. They had become family to her. Some had been with her all five years. They had gone through so much together: contests among themselves, competitions with other lifeguard companies, rescues, even deaths.

So when two senior guards happened to be over at our house one day, my wife and I started talking about throwing a surprise party for Anne's birthday and enlisting their help in inviting the rest of her lifeguard company. I picked one of them to be responsible for spreading the word. It wasn't until the night of the party, when a number of communication snafus almost ruined the evening, that I realized I had misjudged these two guys. I had picked the more outgoing of the two, not realizing the other one was much more reliable and cared the most for people. I might have avoided some hassles had I picked him, but his dark, brooding personality scared me away.

In fact, he had been around our house a few other times that summer, having taken more than a friendly interest in my daughter, and I was somewhat concerned about that. He keeps his thoughts to himself, rarely laughs, and only speaks when spoken to. He's as far back into his own mind as possible, and when he does speak, he tilts his head back as if he's trying to get back farther still. His eyes are thin slits that peer down a short, beaklike nose and his dark skin adds to the mystery. He's the kind of guy you can be around for an evening and never have a clue as to what's going on in his mind. He could be a great person, but "ax murderer" seemed to suit his personality better. Okay, that may be going a little too far, but I couldn't help but wonder what might happen should all those pent-up feelings force their way out.

"So how are you doing?" I asked him after the party was underway.

"I'm very disappointed with who isn't here," he said.

"Believe me, they're going to make up for this; I'll make sure of that."

Uh-oh. Talk like that from a suspected ax murderer sort of gives new meaning to the saying: "Heads are gonna roll. . . ." This comment indicated to me that he had seniority and respect. Had I put him in charge of spreading the word about the surprise party, the results might have been different. One thing I was definitely beginning to realize: This guy has much more going on in his head than I imagined.

Some people don't talk much because they don't want to reveal much of themselves. They are secretive. Some people don't talk much because they don't reveal much of themselves *to someone they don't trust*. They are more protective than secretive. These are the kind of people who are very bad at small talk. They only talk when they decide it's worth it. That night, I found myself privileged to be counted worthy of this man's valuable thoughts, as he embarked on a lengthy discussion about God and the Bible.

He began by commenting on my music. He had heard me play a few times for some of Anne's friends. He had noticed the faith connection in my songs, and he had some questions he wanted to discuss with me. As we talked, I began to suspect his quietness was just a cover for a mind working overtime. The next forty-five minutes confirmed that, as this previously secretive individual suddenly became an open book of thoughts and feelings about life, poetry, literature, and how to relate to God.

I found out that his favorite author is T. S. Eliot, he likes British poets like Thomas Hardy, and he likes stories with unpredictable endings—the kind that throw in a hook at the end. But by far the most surprising part of this conversation was when he related his own religious experience to me.

"I grew up Lutheran but left the church when my pastor didn't have answers for the questions I was asking."

"I bet he didn't," I said, coming to the pastor's defense. "Your questions would have intimidated anyone."

"It would have been fine if he had just admitted that he didn't have the answers," he went on to say, "but he didn't. So I left the church and started reading the Bible for myself and came up with the answers I needed."

"Really? What part?"

"I like the Old Testament the best. Especially the part about Abraham and Isaac. I can't imagine how he could have been willing to give up his son."

"I know; I have two sons." I decided to find out what was in that quiet head of his since he suddenly seemed animated, so I went for a direct question. "How do you suppose Abraham got to the place where he could do that?"

"He believed."

"What do you suppose it was that he believed?" I asked. "What could have possibly given him the confidence to put to death the son of the promise?"

That question seemed to please and intrigue my daughter's friend at the same time.

"I don't know," he finally said, savoring a question he couldn't answer right away. "I'll have to think about that." So we stood there in silence for a while, me and the ax murderer. It was hard because I can't stand silence in a conversation; he didn't seem to mind at all. *Of course,* I thought, *this is where he lives most of the time. Thoughtful inside, barely looking out.*

Then he broke the silence. "Maybe he believed that God would somehow make it right."

"You mean raise Isaac from the dead?"

"Of course. Isn't that what happened to Jesus? It's kind of a theme, don't you think?" he said. Who would have expected this from such a quiet, mysterious guy? We went on to talk about God and Jesus and especially about who Jesus was. Was He a good man or was He the Son of God? I imagined what else might be going on inside this person's very noisy mind.

"What about the Bible?" he asked.

"I find the Bible to be God's Word about everything we need to know in order to know Him. It reveals who God is, who we are, what went wrong with us, and how we can be fixed."

"Do you think we can be fixed?"

"Well, I'm not fixed yet, but I believe that I will be." We went on to talk about Jesus being God's Son and why He needed to be born of Mary and of God without an earthly father screwing up His DNA so He could be the "new Adam," the firstborn of all redeemed creation. That's why Jesus' death means something, since He was a perfect sacrifice. My new friend was the one to come up with most of this stuff, including the "new Adam" part. I was pretty blown away with the light in his mind. All along I thought he was this brooding, depressing person, and it turns out that part of what he was brooding about was whether Jesus was God's Son.

Now Anne has gone back to Colorado, but this lifeguard still comes by. I hurt for him because he's more interested in my daughter than she is in him. But now *I'm* interested in him. While not a fair exchange, I want to know what he's thinking.

You know, I bet a lot of people are like this if I give them half a chance to tell me what they're really thinking. I bet I'd be surprised. I wonder what I've missed in so many other people whom I haven't listened to because I prejudged them as being uninterested—or worse, an ax murderer.

It was a challenge asking this young man questions, though it was downright fascinating to discover what he was thinking. Much better than listening to myself talk. What I don't know is how this story will end. Who knows? It may yet have an unexpected ending, like his favorite stories.

I know now that you can't always read a person like a book; however, you can be sure that we are all living stories with unexpected endings.

CHAPTER ELEVEN
JUST THE SECURITY
GUY

In a newsletter from a friend of mine who serves as chaplain to the athletes at a major university, my eye spotted a paragraph about how he had just had the opportunity to lead the head coach of the football team to Christ. The things my friend quoted the coach as saying were incredibly open and sincere.

I was amazed. I had just seen this team win an important game in relatively dramatic fashion, scoring two touchdowns in the final quarter. As is typical of televised sports, there were numerous close-ups of the coach as the camera tried to capture his reactions to what was happening on the field. He was stoic in his parka, chatting constantly into his headphones as a steady rain pelted the stadium. His team was ranked in the top ten at the time, and no one had expected them to get that far.

I found myself a little surprised at how casually the team chaplain wrote about this man's conversion. We're talking about the head coach of a nationally ranked football team with a 9–2 record—a coach who was already being courted by a number of NFL franchises. This is big time! This should get national coverage! Imagine how many people would be impressed if they knew someone of his stature had become a Christian!

Rereading the opening of the letter, however, I realized I had read it wrong. It wasn't the head coach he was talking about; it was just the team's head of security. Though I knew this shouldn't make any difference, it did. And realizing that it did meant I had to face something ugly about how I weigh the value of personhood.

This is where I could learn something from David Letterman. Mr. Letterman likes to feature ordinary people on his show. And there is something in the way he does this that gives regular folks dignity. He would have the security guy on his show before he'd have the coach. Video cameras would follow the security guy on the job, and on-site with a headset and microphone, he would take us through his laborious security procedures, which would seem kind of dumb and endearing on television, because this is his real world. And just when you were about to think that the security guy was being patronized, he would come up with a very astute observation that, in its simplicity, would cut through all the showbiz hype and make the talking heads (including David himself) look silly. This happens repeatedly. The security guys look normal and well adjusted; Letterman and his famous guests look like clowns.

Looking around this coffee shop right now, I'm trying to grasp the importance of each one of these people sitting near me. This is very hard for me to do. God makes no distinction as to fame or fortune or power. I do. He makes no distinction as to race, religion, or sexual preference. I do. He makes no distinction as to personal attractiveness, deformity, or handicap. I do. He makes no distinction as to hair color, piercings, and dog collars. I do. His love makes no distinction as to faith. I definitely do. I have this big thick line down the middle of my worlds separating the two camps. And it's not even a true spiritual separation. It's a cultural one. I can relax around Christians; I am nervous around everyone else. And now I know I even have a caste system through which I view Christians. When I thought the head coach had become one, it seemed a much bigger deal than when I realized it was the head of security. It meant a real important guy was joining our team. But just the head of security? No big deal.

* * *

I was raised to believe I had a moral obligation to save the world, and that translated into an obligation to proselytize each and every person I met. Failure to do so was to have that person's blood on my hands. In my youth group we enacted scenes in which former classmates would scream at us from hell, "Why didn't you tell me about Jesus while you had the chance?" These were scenes right out of evangelistic talks we all heard at church camp, or tearful confessions around the campfire regarding friends we knew who had died without knowing Christ. At least I think I understand what motivates the hellfire-and-brimstone street preacher in the park all day. My guess is that it's not love—more like the desire for a good night's sleep. So based on all these images and the accompanying guilt, I can look around this coffee shop right now and feel responsible for everyone here. If I don't say anything, I'm tacitly condemning everyone here to hell. Shall I stand up and start preaching? You can see how difficult this becomes. In my lifetime, I'm only going to end up telling a few people I meet about Jesus. What does that say for everyone else?

It's no wonder that people might feel uneasy around me: I am either condemning them or feeling guilty for not saving them. Simply being a friend to someone who isn't a Christian is not an option for me.

I think about this and have to conclude that a good deal of evangelism is nothing short of abuse. I think it's abusive to make others your project. I think it's abusive to make them the target of your evangelical strategy. I think it's abusive to blame non-Christians for your guilt, merely because they exist. I think it's abusive to make other people a means to an end.

Human life is an end in itself. God made everyone in His image, so things like worth and the value of personhood are intrinsic to all of us regardless of race, religion, nationality, or the status of our salvation. I can embrace my neighbors and seek to understand their culture and their ways. I can work, live, love, and laugh with the people around me and appreciate them as valuable contributors to my life without having to dissect their religious affiliation or spiritual status. I can sit and talk with them over coffee and come to value their journey.

Besides, the famous-people-becoming-Christians-so-everyone-else-will-follow idea never really works. Look at Jane Fonda and Bob Dylan. There was a time when I would have thought that if celebrities became believers, the sky would fall in—or at least hordes of their followers would join the team as well. I figured it would trigger a mass conversion. Well, Jane Fonda and Bob Dylan said they became Christians, and so far, the only people I can tell who have been eternally affected by this have been . . . Jane Fonda and Bob Dylan. And that's pretty significant. It's right up there with the security guard for the university football team being born-again, which is right up there with you and me being born.

CHAPTER TWELVE
DON'T DREAM IT'S OVER

With a tall latte sitting next to my laptop at a
Starbucks in Elgin, Illinois, I was ready to write. It was
an hour and a half before closing time, and I was glad
the store was not crowded. Except for a table of six
college students sitting outside and two employees
behind the counter taking mostly drive-through orders,
I was alone. I was sitting near a wall plug by the window,
so I was set. There would be few distractions, except for
the music track playing hits from the eighties.

A hauntingly familiar melody captured my attention,
and I recognized the Crowded House hit "Don't Dream
It's Over."[3] I've always been intrigued by this song, and
with a newer, cleaner version of it popularized by

Sixpence None the Richer, I've felt new access to lyrics I formerly passed off as being too esoteric for my attention span.

A line from the first verse, which talks about catching something in a paper cup, distracts me. . . .

Just minutes before, I had ordered my latte in a paper cup and snapped the lid on tight. There's something preferable about having my coffee hidden. I like to hold it surreptitiously in my hand. I take it this way, even when I'm drinking it in a coffeehouse and could have it in one of those colorful, big ceramic mugs with the foam piled high. I prefer the paper cup, partly because the lid helps keep it hot longer and partly because the paper lends a certain aroma to the coffee that now accompanies my finer coffee experiences. Gourmet coffee in a paper cup. It works for me. There's something about the cup, the cardboard collar that shields your hand from the heat, and the lid that seals in all that flavor and delivers it with pinpoint accuracy through the little hole in the top.

It appeared that the university students on the patio outside were having too much fun to realize I was watching them. They were so close—only feet from me—but we were separated by thick plate glass that completely shut out the sound of their voices. We were in two worlds, side by side, yet separated by an invisible wall. I watched their lips move, I watched them laugh, but I couldn't hear the joke.

On the table next to me was a copy of that day's *Chicago Tribune*. The headlines were no joke at all. They

told the number of Americans who had been killed in
Iraq since American and British troops entered that
country in the spring 2003—this particular headline
announced that more Americans had died since taking
over the country than in the actual battle to overtake it.

*And with a strange prophetic accuracy, the lyrics of the
Crowded House song mention the waste of war and the way
we can blow it all off so easily merely by selecting another
show on television. . . .*

The dissonance in the lyrics mimicked the dissonance
I felt as I sat peacefully drinking a latte while newspaper
images of someone's world being blown to bits assaulted
my insulated self. The loss and complete upheaval of
everything in life that war brings is something I cannot
even begin to fathom. War has come closer to Americans
since the events of 9/11, and yet I still struggle with a
kind of disconnect. I travel so much that I can gauge the
intensity of the terrorism threat by the amount of time it
takes to get through airport security on any given day.
With each international incident everything tightens, and
then it slowly loosens over time. But like it or not, the
news media brings a violent world right to our window
every day, and we have to decide if we are going to
embrace it. We watch the lips move on our TV screen,
but the cries of anguish are unintelligible from this side
of the glass.

I wondered about a bomb going off inside some
zealot's parka in a nice coffee shop like this one in Bagh-
dad or Jerusalem. I wondered how long it will be before

it happens here in America. I noticed that a sweatshirt on one of the girls out on the patio looked a little bulky, but that was just because it was cool outside. *Still*, I thought, *wouldn't it be the perfect terrorist strategy to blow up a Starbucks in Elgin, Illinois?* No one would ever feel safe again anywhere in America.

This glass would not protect me from a bomb, but it would protect me from an encounter with these kids, and just then I welcomed that. Most of the time, I would rather observe people than interact with them. I tell myself this is part of being a writer, though I use this much too often as an excuse to stay isolated. I am a sociologist—a social-philosopher—I have a right to people-watch. But the true value of personhood comes more through encounter than through mere observation. Still, there is a place and a time for both, and I didn't feel guilty about ignoring the kids out there.

I wasn't even tempted to indulge in any "evangelical guilt" over them. (That's what a Christian feels in the presence of strangers who probably aren't Christians and whose only chance to hear the gospel might be through me right now. If I ignore that fact, I am in essence condemning them to their doom.) Even if I were to indulge in this guilt, it would have been in vain, since the girl with the bulky sweatshirt—the potential suicide bomber—turned my way and I saw that her sweatshirt sported the name of a local Christian college. See, they were probably all Christians anyway.

And what does any of this have to do with

personhood and the worth of the individual? Nothing. Absolutely nothing. The person who goes to hell is just as valuable as the person who goes to heaven. Therein lies the tragedy and the really big question for God that I don't think any of us can adequately answer, though we make an attempt. I'm sure not going to try, especially since I am finally getting it about the intrinsic value of being born. I'm not in the least bit interested in condemning anyone anywhere, and I am totally relieved to know that this is not and will never be my job. I do know it's my job, however, to appreciate what God has made in His own image.

Once in a while (and not often enough) I get a glimpse of the enormous value represented by just one human being—the hopes and dreams, and the intertwining relationships of love and hate, truth and lies, that make up one person's life. When I multiply that by the billions of people on the face of the earth, the implications are too staggering to contain, like staring into the night sky trying to take in the enormity of the universe. I try and fail, then return to my own little issues in life and miss the small continent that is each person on the little circle of the globe around which I roam. And every one of those people has his or her own issues that are, in that person's view, more important than mine. It's good for me to remember that.

I thought about the kids on the other side of the glass and realized that their greatest asset was that they were simply and profoundly born; they deserved to be appreciated for that. Each kid was a whole book of feelings, hopes, dreams, and disappointments.

Fred Rogers (of *Mister Rogers' Neighborhood*) used to talk about how he always felt like bowing in the presence of others because he knew he was sharing in something sacred. "As different as we are from one another, as unique as each one of us is, we are much more the same than we are different."[4] I can remember a time when I had doubts about Mister Rogers precisely for statements like this, because he evoked such universality in his acceptance of all people. "To love someone is to strive to accept that person exactly the way he or she is, right here and now."[5] This runs counter to the erroneous theology of my experience that taught me that the world was made up of good people and bad people. How can you accept someone without finding out first whether he or she is one of the good people? And wouldn't the blanket acceptance of a bad person condone his or her badness?

Of course, Mister Rogers always took care of these problems by including everyone in the all-encompassing *we*. Mister Rogers spent his life teaching people how to break down walls so that we could experience the fact that we are all neighbors.

And wouldn't you know it, the lyrics of the chorus of the song still playing—the most familiar part of the song—are all about people who are trying to build walls between others and how we can't let them succeed. . . .

I am ready to conclude that there is no "them." I know better now. I am made of the same stuff, banished from the same garden, groveling on the same earth, locked in the same struggles as anyone. We have more in common than not. We sin. We lose. We rationalize. We laugh. We judge. We condemn. We cry and blow bubbles. And, yes, we might even like our coffee strong with a good deal of hot milk steamed into it and delivered in a paper cup with a cardboard sleeve and a hole in the top. Or maybe not. Either way it's okay.

So, in the words of the dearly beloved Mister Rogers, "Won't you be my neighbor?" No time for fresh paint on any of our lives, just throw open the window to our heart and wipe our eyes clear. Come to the door of my heart and please come in. I welcome you. You'll have to step over my imperfect self, but let's walk before the Christ who loves us both unconditionally—just the way we are.

And there's that song again—talking now about liberation and relief and about getting closer and closer to someone's heart. . . .

It appears to me, at least in my experience, that our differences are much more easily recognized than our similarities are. It's much easier to hate what is different than to find what is shared and embrace it. Prejudice seems to spring naturally from our fallen nature. Overcoming it can be a daunting assignment. Attitudes, like walls, are built over time, but the good news is that walls come down much faster than they are built.

Everyone appreciates being treated decently; everyone likes to have fun. We all want to feel part of something bigger than ourselves. At the end of the day, it's much more significant to realize how similar we are as human beings than how different we *think* we might be.

What do others see when they see me? It's okay; I can laugh at myself. "Why didn't you tell me my tie had a stain dribbling down the middle or that I had whipped cream on the tip of my nose?" Bob Dylan once sang about his desire to have me stand inside his shoes so I could find out what a drag it is to see me. And when I think of it that way, it probably is a drag to see me—at least when I am into myself. Ironically, those are the times when I need this perspective the most.

Who is the wall builder? It has to be me. Nobody else cares as much about my self-preservation as I do. It is also my desire to keep everything unknown out. Stay with what I know—what is comfortable and safe. Stay only with those who believe as I do. Differences threaten. But differences also sharpen beliefs and cut out what is unnecessary. And differences always lead to something in common.

I am not suggesting we all blend our heartfelt beliefs and our understanding of ourselves into some postmodern mix. Rather, I am recommending we concentrate on what makes someone else's heart beat, and in so doing, recognize our own driving passion. Discover together how wonderfully made we are in the image of God and how much we long to be loved and to love. It is an act of vulnerability that can be frightening but well worth making.

This is an adventure that we travel together. I do not think we ever really arrive—we just gather more travelers as we go along. Thank heaven for places to stop along the way and reflect and interact— especially over coffee. The truth is discovered along the road as much as it will be in the arrival at our destination.

And the song plays on . . . something about battles won and lost, and never seeing the end of the road. . . .

Don't dream it's over, because it's not.

CHAPTER THIRTEEN
SILENT SCREAMS

"In 1971, at the age of nineteen, I discovered I was pregnant. Total panic set in. This problem had to be taken care of, I told myself. It had to go away. My first and only thought was of my parents and their reaction. They must never find out. I knew that they would disown me."

Curled up on our couch, feeling lost and very sad, the woman's only comfort came from the hot mug of coffee she clung to as if someone might wrestle even this from her grasp. She struggled to explain why she felt so emotionally spent.

"I remember the cold table," she continued, "the stirrups, the loud machinery, the pain, because this time I was awake. Next, I'm curled up on my living-room floor by myself, crying and feeling very sad, lonely, ashamed, confused, and empty. I cried all night but didn't know why I was crying, or for whom."

Her problem was supposed to have been taken care of back then, when she and those around her were convinced abortion was the best solution to a difficult situation. It was just "a blob of tissue" anyway. At least that's what the nurse told her.

"So why do I still feel so depressed after all these years?"

A staunch pro-life advocate in her church, this woman is a secret sufferer—one of every three women in evan- gelical churches has had at least one abortion.[6] Who does this woman share her life's pain with? No one. And every time pro-life supporters—herself among them—speak about the harm of abortion, her wounds are opened again. Over the years, the guilt and torment have mounted inside as her silent screams drive her painful contradictions further inside her.

She loves God and she knows God loves her, even though she feels unlovely. She has received His accep- tance, but she is convinced no one from the fellowship of her church would ever forgive her—never mind love her—if they were to find out the truth about her.

Sometimes coffee is a person's only friend.

That's why she was sitting on our couch. In the security of my wife's acceptance, she was beginning to open up.

I acted as if I were trying to understand what was going on here—pretending to lend my support—but I seemed

to be missing the full impact of the situation. I got the
Kleenex (I am a willing servant, often covering my own
conflict with mundane activity) but I felt detached. I didn't
relate well to my wife's pain during childbirth—how can I
connect to this baby's death so long ago? My wife has told
me how I was present in body but somewhere else
emotionally during her pregnancies. I felt the same pulling
away now. I wanted this little session to be over. I wanted
to get on with my evening. I resented the intrusion of
someone else's inner pain.

On top of that, I was missing a good ball game on TV.
I wondered what team was up and if there were any
runners on base.

Marti, however, lives for moments like this, and I
could sense her intensity growing. I was pushing away
what she was embracing. She warmed her hands as
though readying herself for what was to come.

Now she moved things along by suggesting I go over
and put my arm around this woman and hold her. Marti
knew full well what I was doing, why I was trying to get
away. She knew I couldn't embrace this woman without
embracing my own sin, and I was not very good at that.
It was certainly not that I didn't sin; it was just that . . .
well . . . okay, I'll come out and say it: My sin wasn't
quite as bad as hers. The big rub, if I'm totally honest, is
that I'm willing to admit I'm a sinner, just not a really
bad one. She was lower than me on the totem pole of
sin. I'd embrace her, but I have to come down the pole
to get to her. What I'd really like are levels of grace,

please, so I can stay with what I consider the not-so-bad sinners yet still be forgiven. People could know I was bad, just not *that* bad.

So I moved over next to her on the couch, but my arms stayed at my side.

"I turned over my life to God, all except one area—one door," she continued. "That door was very tightly locked—locked so tight that my memories were just about gone. I called myself pro-choice back then. To say or think anything else would have been admitting the impossible. The idea that I had killed my child was too painful. Denial continued to be very strong, but fortunately so was Jesus' love and grace."

And here I was going to hand her my grace card and go check out the ball game, but it looked like she already had one with lots of room on it. That meant I had to relate to her as my sister in Christ.

Marti knew me so well. That's why she was pushing us together, as if to say, "Go ahead. Crawl into each other's pain. Grace will find you."

"I even became quite active in my church," the woman said, too absorbed in her own struggle to have a clue about mine. "Not only was I going to be the best mom in the world, but now I was going to be the best church woman also, doing many good and important things. But the busier I got at church, the more friends I had, the lonelier and trashier I felt. I worked harder, but I knew I was garbage."

Now I was thinking about our church and realized

that it was full of people like me who had signed an unwritten pact to avoid the shame of confessing our sin, so we could keep on pretending we didn't have any. Suddenly I saw the tragedy of this situation. This woman was dying of thirst right next to the fountain of grace, but because no one was dipping into that grace for their own life, no one had any to share with her. We were choking off the flow of the very river that washed each of us clean every hour, every minute.

I knew there was no difference between this woman and me, but it was one thing to know that in my head and another to embrace her and share her position. I wanted to keep her as the needy one. I wanted to stay her counselor.

I found myself moving closer and putting my arm around her. This caused her to cry more. I reached for more Kleenex, feeling awkward. Marti was smiling. Suddenly the counselee had an arm around the counselor, and tears were working their way into my eyes now. I fought them, trying to hold them back. My arms were telling her that everything was going to be okay. Strangely, her hold on me was telling me the same. A tangible healing was going on. I was holding onto a self-convicted murderer, and suddenly I saw the shame of my own loss, one sinner to another. The closer I got to her pain, the more I felt mine.

I decided I could use some of her coffee.

For so long this woman was secretly among the walking wounded—a post-abortive woman from my church, now on my couch, finding her way into my opening heart. She always looked so great, nicely dressed, and all together. She fooled us all. I thought I had the corner on hiding what I did not think others would accept. Now we acknowledged to each other that we were both experts at this—from the sin on through to the cover-up. I was taking in all that I could.

How long had I walked as though I had no sin? How far had I gone into hiding out of fear that another Christian would point a bony finger in my face, sending me away in scorn with each truthful word spoken? How brave this woman was to be willing to step out from behind her shame, her denial, and to step into her fear and face me—the one she probably thought would be the first to throw stones at her in condemnation.

How brave of me, thank you, to face her—to back down the totem pole to where I belong. Years ago I wrote these lines in a song: "You don't sin alone; we are all one in the Lord." I think I know what that means now. If we are all in this sin soup together, there is no degree of separation between us. I cannot call her sin worse than mine and separate myself from her. Of course, this means we're in on the good stuff together too.

I sensed something changing in me that night. I hoped her life was changing too. Forgiveness was set in motion that evening. Christ died for her sin and mine. Thank goodness our sins were not too much for Him.

Suddenly, some barrier between Marti's friend and me had come down. I hardly cared what the score was between us—or in the game I had wanted to watch. I'd find out soon enough in the morning paper. The score here was two to nothing: Two sinners reduced to nothing resulted in a win for each of us. After all, we were on the same team anyway.

"Would you like some more coffee?" I asked her. "Because I think I would like to join you."

CHAPTER FOURTEEN
FROM STEEPLES
TO ST. ARBUCKS

Once it was a church that signaled a town's rite of passage; now it's a Starbucks.

I lived in one of the earliest settlements in Massachusetts for seven years—a town of steeples, Federalist sea captains' homes along High Street, and memories of the tall ships that once graced a harbor more spacious than Boston's. Those steeples authenticated the community of Newburyport as early as 1635. About 350 years later, it was a McDonald's just off Interstate 95 that said Newburyport had arrived. And now, sometime during the twelve years since we moved away, sure enough, a Starbucks has moved in downtown. We've gone from

"Praise God from whom all blessings flow" to "One nonfat vanilla latte, extra hot, please" as a sign of civic success.

Talk of steeples always reminds me of the riddle we would act out as kids in church. With hands clasped and fingers tucked in—all except for the index fingers that pressed together to form a steeple and thumbs held together for the front door—we would say, "Here's the church, here's the steeple, open the door—" and we'd pull open our hands to reveal interlocking, wiggling fingers— "and look at all the people." Then we'd repeat the riddle but with fingers clasped normally over our knuckles: "Here's the church, here's the steeple, open the door and—" opening to nothing but empty palms—"where are all the people?" Of course numerous theories abounded as to where the people were, from "They've all gone home" to my favorite, "They're all on the roof sunbathing."

So during a church service recently, I was surprised to find the riddle still alive. The pastor used it as part of his children's sermon, and when he got to the "Where are all the people?" part, a five-year-old's hand shot up immediately, begging to be called upon.

"Yes, Heather," he said, pointing to her. "Where are all the people?"

"They're at Starbucks," she said to a surprised congregation. The little girl might have been joking, but there is much truth in her reply. In many ways, the corner coffee shop has picked up where the corner church left off, not only as the new indicator of commercial viability, but as a place where the real spiritual needs of people can be addressed one-on-one over coffee.

Where do you go to be with a group of people who share something in common and accept you for who you are, no questions asked? Where do you go where you know you will be treated equally and with respect? Where do you go when you're down-and-out and need a friend? Where do you go when you just want to be around some warm bodies? Where do you go—and I can hear the theme song from *Cheers* now—"where everybody knows your name"? Well, there's a better chance of finding all these things in a Starbucks than in a church.

That's because so many people believe the myth that being a regular church member means your life is, by and large, under control. If you have any problems they are on the mend and don't merit much discussion. It's something of an unspoken assumption that it is okay to be a sinner if you haven't been saved; but once you are born-again, sin should stay hidden. People can't let on to the fact that they are not living a "victorious Christian life." Everyone is pretty busy being good.

I will tell you a secret. Despite what it might look like on the surface, the people in church on Sunday are just as afraid as anybody. They are isolated within themselves, hoping no one will recognize the sorry state they live within—the stuff no one can see.

In our isolation, we all peer out from within, dying for someone to truly engage in us—in our good, our bad, and our ugly moments. For until someone does—until someone embraces us out of the mercy of God—we will all go on feeling judged, unwanted, and worthless in ourselves.

Enter St. Arbucks, another kind of church. I actually have heard of a group of guys who treat their local Starbucks like a church, gathering there weekly to fellowship, study the Bible, and pray. That's how they came up with this new name: St. Arbucks. Sounds like a mainline church, doesn't it? Like one of those old stone structures with a steeple you'd expect to find on a downtown street corner.

Something about this seems right and perhaps more of what church needs to be. Having church over coffee will always be more interpersonally engaging than having church in a church. You can avoid everyone there, but you can't avoid someone across the table wanting to know how your day went.

There's also the perceived problem of everyone in church avoiding you, and more often than not, they really do. You get more attention at Starbucks—and more respect. As a customer, you get the full treatment; as a visitor in church, you are an outsider. Some churches can be as closed as a country club.

If church were more like St. Arbucks, would more people want to go? It is interesting that many larger churches today have put in coffee bars. Some even have a seating area just like a coffee bar's. Maybe they are finding out what the guys at St. Arbucks already know.

Church needs to change. The whole point of what

Jesus did for us on the cross was to make it possible for us all to come forward and be honest about our life—to get ourselves out in the open and in the light of God's revealing truth to be both exposed and forgiven—to mourn our sin and celebrate our salvation over and over again. Who wouldn't be welcome in a place full of people astonished over their own forgiveness and grateful for God's grace and mercy toward them day by day?

Would you come to church if the people there were overjoyed to see you, regardless of your state, because they saw themselves as the worst of sinners and were eager to extend to everyone the mercy God had extended to them? Would more people come to church if they knew no one would judge them, because everyone there was so aware of his own brokenness that he couldn't possibly point a finger at someone else? Or maybe it isn't about more people coming as much as it is that a different kind of person would come if church were like this: a meeting of people willing to come into the light together and receive God's forgiveness.

I remember walking out of church on sunny Sunday mornings as a child and being temporarily blinded by the intense brightness of daylight bouncing off the front of the church with its white columns and concrete steps. It always took awhile for my eyes to adjust. Isn't it odd that you walk out of church and go from darkness into light?

CHAPTER FIFTEEN
MESSAGE
IN A BOTTLE

You can fool some of the people all of the time and all of the people some of the time, but you can never fool your wife. I know that's not the way the saying goes, but it's the truth.

The next two chapters are a glimpse into two marriages: my own marriage and that of a dear couple, Horton and Edna Voss (both now passed away), who were my example of what marriage can be. Believe me, I have tried to make my story come out better than it does here, but those attempts never get by my primary critic, who for this book happens to be my wife. Men should be able to talk about their marriage without their wife around. The story comes out so much better that way, but my wife has no stomach for facade, especially as a Christian on record—one of the main reasons for the caffeinated nature of these revelations. I could never be this honest on decaf.

* * *

"Look at that bottle, or whatever it is," I said as I noticed the large, plastic object washed ashore down on the beach in front of our hotel room. "That looks like the same thing I saw floating around out there during dinner."

"I saw it too," said Marti. "Maybe it's a bottle with a message in it for you."

A spotlight from the hotel illumined the water in the early evening darkness, and Marti's eyes were as bright as the lit-up beach. Now the thought that there might actually be a personal message in a bottle out there probably seems a bit far-fetched, but you have to realize that this is the same woman who broke her collarbone at the early age of five, believing she could fly around the room like Wendy, John, and Michael in *Peter Pan* if she concentrated on happy thoughts. One would think an abrupt and painful encounter with the floor from her top bunk would have brought her to her senses, but, no, she continues undaunted in her belief in magical things. It is her faith in the impossible that makes it real. If Marti said there might be a message out there for me, I knew I had better check it out.

"Lord, make it magical," she pleaded, as I headed for

the beach. We both knew we were in desperate need of something to keep us from pulling away from each other. We had come to this beach resort to reevaluate our relationship and hopefully to reconnect with what was important in a stressful time.

✳ ✳ ✳

We have the most creative and volatile relationship of any couple I know. We are alike in that we are both emotional, though in completely opposite directions: Marti's emotions drive her outward; mine drive me inward.

Marti is socially dominant. She loves the sense of immediacy she gets from being engaged fully in life. She does not have much patience with lukewarm responses or halfhearted actions from others. And while she has the vision, compassion, and heart to be a tremendous influence for good, this desire to be vital and alive can easily deteriorate into a need to constantly push against the world—and especially me. She can be like a person who insists on continually pushing a door marked "Pull" (which shows how much attention she pays to directions, by the way). Her intensity either provides me with an extremely accurate insight about my potential and life's possibilities or overwhelms me so much I look for opportunities to avoid her.

I, on the other hand, am emotionally dominant because of an acute awareness of my feelings about myself and other people. As a creative person, this means I can express the personal and the universal—transforming my experience into something valuable for those seeking a deeper understanding of who they are. But often in my attempt to understand my own inner reality, I go deeper into myself and stay there, just to avoid Marti's forceful energy. Then I usually imagine lengthy conversations between the two of us, particularly if the feelings are negative or resentful toward her. I know these mental conversations are essentially unreal and at best only rehearsals for action, but I prefer rehearsal to engagement.

Thus our life together is a push and tug—a quest for control. Where our strengths and weaknesses are so close, we have formed a protective shell against the weaker qualities. Hostilities often bubble up between us as we seek to get a reaction from each other's storminess. The question is, what kind of a reaction are we seeking?

At our best, we fulfill what is lacking in each other's personality and outlook; at our worst . . . well, think Peter O'Toole and Katharine Hepburn as Henry II and his estranged wife, Eleanor of Aquitaine, in the classic film *The Lion in Winter*: "What shall we hang?" Eleanor asks, as the stormy pair contemplate the coming Christmas. "The holly, or each other?"

✳ ✳ ✳

I approached the object on the beach, walking on the sand, feeling the cool spray of the waves on my face. As I got closer I saw it was not a bottle after all, but a balloon—a partially deflated Mylar balloon.

The disappointment from discovering that it was not a bottle was short-lived. As I got closer, I noticed the writing was not in it but on it. As I picked it up, the weight of the message hit me powerfully as each word/picture gave way to deeply personal implications. First, there was a picture of Tinker Bell, Marti's hero, creating a star with her wand. Then there was the message—a birthday greeting that I couldn't immediately make out because some of the lettering had been washed away. But when I saw it was a birthday balloon, I realized that part was for me. It was my birthday.

"What is it?" she called from the balcony.

"Oh, nothing," I called back. "Just a balloon—a birthday balloon—with Tinker Bell on it!"

She clapped her hands like a child. "Oh, let me see!"

I returned to the room beaming, holding the balloon up as a trophy, yet trying to control my joy for fear the bubble might burst. But there it was in print: "Have a Magical Birthday!"

No message could have been more confirming. This balloon had been purchased by some parent and released by some birthday child probably ten or twenty miles away. It had been carried by the winds over the ocean where it sank into the sea. It must have floated for some time because a good deal of the color had worn off. Then the balloon slowly made its way to shore to kiss the dolphins and capture our attention at sunset. Finally, it came to rest directly beneath our balcony and stayed there until later that night when we went out for some fresh air and saw it.

Marti saw it as an opportunity to fan the gleam of hope in my eye and recapture the energy that had fired up our relationship in the beginning. I saw it as God's confirmation of all I had discovered that day, as I went back and reaffirmed my love and commitment to my wife. This was a bona fide magical miracle and almost as good as flying around the room.

It's a good thing because I needed a miracle. I had made promises to my wife that weekend, but promises always come down to the here and now.

"How will you know when I'm out of my small place?" I asked Marti. (I like the small place that demands little of me and has few resources available. I like this because I feel less likely to fail, and I have less to be responsible for.)

"You'll know," she said. "You don't need me for that."

CHAPTER SIXTEEN
ROSES ON
WEDNESDAY

"**S**omeday I'm going to write a book about you and Horton," I said while Edna puttered among the flower-pots, checking soil with a small trowel.

"Nonsense," she protested. "What could you possibly say about Horton and me that would be worth writing down?"

"Plenty," I said.

"What great thing have we accomplished? We've merely lived an ordinary life."

"Ah, but that's just it," I said, watching her move up and down the rows of new rose plants like a treasured flower herself, bloomed and curling. Peach-colored skin and thick apricot hair, which she kept cropped a little shaggy, defied her age. She was small of stature, putting her face at the same height as some of the taller buds.

"You've lived your life so far in an extraordinary way. That's a greater accomplishment than merely doing extraordinary things."

"Well, wait till I'm gone, then, so I don't have to read it."

"Why? What could be so bad about your story in print?"

"There's nothing to write about, dear."

"What about the roses Horton brings you on Wednesdays? That's a story worth telling."

A smile came over her face when I said it, like some great secret had just been divulged. She stopped for a minute and focused her eyes on a full, clear pink flower. Cupping it with her gloved hands, she turned it in my direction. "Would you look at that beauty?"

"Exquisite," I said.

"This is my 'Billy Graham' bush and I think it's about ready to be planted."

"You named a rosebush after an evangelist?"

"No. The grower did. It's a new hybrid. That white one over there is a 'John F. Kennedy.'"

"Billy Graham I can understand, but I'm surprised you'd allow a Democrat in your garden."

"They're not all bad, dear," she said with a wink.

"You must have a 'Ronald Reagan' here somewhere then," I said, surveying rows of plants in their greenhouse and knowing Edna's political leanings.

"Not yet, but I will soon—as soon as someone invents one."

I kept the next comment about inventing Ronald Reagan to myself. Horton and Edna had always loved roses. Their backyard in Redlands, California, rivaled a presidential rose garden, and the greenhouse that Horton built behind the garage was Edna's favorite place to spend time. It was where they nursed new plants before moving them into the yard. Edna kept abreast of the latest developments in rose horticulture and couldn't resist the exotic new hybrids that kept showing up in mail-order catalogs.

"So Horton told you about roses on Wednesday, did he? How did that come up?"

"I asked him. I wanted to know if there were any secrets to your happy marriage, something I could use in mine."

"Don't call it a happy marriage, please," she said, knocking on the wooden table Horton built for the potted plants. "Sounds like a commercial for success. We don't have the perfect marriage."

"You have the best one I know of, by far."

"You haven't been around very long, have you? We have nothing of the kind."

Never able to receive compliments well, Edna shook her gardening trowel at me with a sly, little smile. "You single us out and you're making a big mistake."

"How many husbands do you know who bring their wives roses on Wednesday just because they're thinking about them?" I asked.

"Well . . . Horton *is* special."

I wanted to prod her about the roses. Horton hadn't given me much. "Tell me about the roses, then. I promise I won't write it down, at least not now. When did they start coming? Does he do this every Wednesday? Come on, Edna, tell me some stories." I knew I had her. She loved to talk about Horton, and I caught a glimpse of that look in her eye that signaled a great tale brewing.

Edna laid down her trowel and came over to where I was sitting, wagging her head as she walked. She removed her muddy gardening gloves finger by finger as if they matched an evening gown, dropping them one at a time on the table. "All right, come inside; I'm sure the coffee is ready now. 'But of many books there is no end, and much study wearies the body.' That's King Solomon, you know, and you'd better think about that before you clutter the library with another book no one needs to read."

✻ ✻ ✻

It was mid-June, midweek, midmorning of a beautiful day in Redlands, nine years after my visit with Edna in her greenhouse. Edna had to run to the store on an errand. She found Horton in the newly constructed room off the garage that was well on its way to becoming his coveted painting studio. Many of his land- and seascapes graced their spacious, Spanish-style home on Highland

Avenue. Now, in the first month of his retirement, he was looking forward to finally having a permanent place to create his works of art with proper lighting and a view of their fine rose garden.

"I wish you'd listen to me and let the house painters paint this room while they're here," she said.

"Nothing doing," he said with eyes twinkling. "This room has been in my mind too long. I don't want anyone painting these walls who doesn't pour love into every inch." And the woman into whom he had poured every inch of his love for forty years gave him a kiss as she left for the corner store. They never parted, even for a short trip like this, without kissing.

The garage door rose on two Jaguar XKE sports cars, identical except for their color. Edna got into the white one and backed down the long driveway. It was indicative of Horton's love for her that he would not have such a button of a sports car without his wife having one, too, even if only for tooling around town.

They had lived in this house for fifteen years and built a solid place in the community. Edna taught and served on the board of Bible Study Fellowship. Horton served as a deacon in their church and on two overseas missions boards. Their gracious home had well accommodated the groups they had both served, providing a hospitable place for entertaining and a home away from home for single young adults whom they periodically took under their wing to nurture and give back to the church at large.

As soon as Edna was gone, Horton went out to the garden and cut three of the finest new buds off their 'Crimson Glory' hybrid tea rosebush. Inside the house, he put them in a vase and left it on the kitchen counter next to a note on which he had written: "It's Wednesday . . ." It was the only time in forty years that he had not delivered the roses in person. He must have known, somehow, that he would not be able to do so that day.

Edna returned from her brief trip and called to Horton from the garage to help her with a few things. The studio was attached to the back wall of the garage and accessed by a door that was partly open. When Horton did not respond, she assumed he was inside the house. She struggled with two sacks of groceries, leaving one behind, and called to him from the kitchen. There was still no answer, so she went upstairs and checked their bedroom.

"Horton," she called. Even hearing Edna say his name was to understand a little about their relationship. She always said it with a certain playfulness in her voice. The syllables danced—probably because Horton had made her dance for forty years. Always full of surprises, he would look at her with a continual glimmer in his eyes, as if, after all these years, he still had something up his sleeve that she didn't know about. She, in turn, had been surprised so many times, that whenever she said his name, it sounded as if she had just been caught by his charm yet one more time.

By the time she returned to the garage, however, the

charm had gone out of her voice and an urgency had replaced it, and when she uttered the final "HORTON!" upon finding her beloved on the floor of his unfinished studio, the sound of her gut-wrenching cry sent workers running from the main house. They attempted CPR. They called 911. The paramedics came only to pronounce the obvious. Once they arrived and pried Edna away, they did not let her near the body again. They were never forgiven.

Twenty minutes later, upstairs in her room, the family doctor was attempting to comfort Edna, a task that was not easy for him since he was a longtime friend who cared very much for them both. As he held her, trying to cushion her sobbing, Edna went down on her knees with grief and leaned against her bed.

"I hurt," was all she could manage to say.

"Of course you do," said the doctor, stooping down to meet her.

"No! I HURT!"

Suddenly the doctor observed Edna more carefully and realized instantly that she, too, was having a heart attack. It was inevitable to everyone who knew them and had observed their deep and lasting love for each other: The two had become one, and their ties could not be severed without physical as well as emotional pain. So on the floor of her bedroom, Edna assumed the position she had found her husband in only thirty minutes earlier and fought *not* to respond to those who were coaxing her back to life.

* * *

After Horton's death I first saw Edna in the hospital. Over the phone the day before, she had alarmed me by stating that she was struggling over whether to live or die.

"Edna, you wouldn't . . ." I had said, assuming she was contemplating the worst. After a battery of tests, the doctors had found no physical evidence of a heart attack. Edna's emotional loss was so great, it had put her through all the real symptoms of a heart attack without her actually suffering one. The doctors said they had never seen anything like it.

"I wouldn't need to *do* anything, dear," she had said over the phone. "I would just will myself dead. I can, you know." And I knew she could. That's why I had decided to travel to Redlands before hearing any word about a service. No one was even thinking about a service yet, with Edna's condition in the balance.

But it wasn't only Edna who brought me. It was my own memories, and the need to return one last time to their home. These people were real. You could touch everything here: their faith, their love for each other, their enjoyment of life . . . such a rare combination that in my adulthood I was only beginning to find out how rare. I had even gotten a chance to be in the house briefly after my arrival, while no one was there—alone with my memories. That's when I found the roses still in the kitchen, right where Horton had left them.

It's easy to understand how they could have been missed; no one else would have known the significance. Roses on Wednesday had been my secret with Horton. It was nothing they ever broadcast, even to their children. It was my job to deliver this final bouquet—and perhaps was even my story to tell. Horton or Edna would never tell it. His death was way too soon for me. I felt a huge loss as I walked through that empty house, hearing my footsteps echo off the wood floors. I was old enough to know how few men like Horton there are in the world, and I wasn't anywhere near finished receiving what I felt I needed from him. A sure, steady presence was gone from my life, and even though I had not seen Horton and Edna in a number of years, just the knowledge that he was there meant something to me.

This was why I had the vase of roses and Horton's note with me when I walked into Edna's room in the hospital.

The late afternoon sun sliced through the venetian blinds and fell in stripes across the hospital bed. The only sounds were the methodic beeping of a heart monitor breaking the low hum of the air-conditioning. Edna, hardly recognizable, lay motionless, arms at her sides, their weight pulling the bedsheets tightly around her. Stainless-steel bars encased her bed, clinical and passionless. I marveled at how her face held its sixty-five years proudly with a degree of protest against time and the cold reality that now waited outside the thin membranes of her dark eyelids. She'd always had a ruddy face with deep lines that signaled her ready laughter. But now, lines I had never seen before pulled at her face.

Her hair stood in short tufts, its rusty orange running solid to the roots. She would not approve of the way it looked. Her fingernails, which had recently been done (they always were), now showed just a few remaining streaks of the pumpkin color that had been removed by a nurse, who needed to keep an eye on the color under her nails. She would not be happy about this either. Black wires extended up from under her arms and shoulders and trailed over the steel bars like a huge science-fiction spider pinning her down to the bed.

"Edna," I said, leaning close to her ear. I repeated her name.

"Go away. I told you, I don't want to live."

"Edna, it's me, John."

"John?" she said raising her eyebrows without opening her eyes. "What in the Sam Hill are you doing here?"

"I came to see you."

"Go home. There's nothing to see."

"Edna, I'm so sorry. I don't know what to say."

"Then, for heaven's sake, don't say anything at all."

Even though there was a faint glow starting to show on her cheeks as she recognized my voice, silence was what she wanted, and that was what worried me. What was going on in her head couldn't be good. She needed people in her life now—other reasons to live, now that her primary one was gone.

Edna opened her eyes and immediately noticed the vase of roses in my hand.

"Where did you get those?" she said. "They look just like my 'Crimson Glorys.'"

"They are," I said, handing her Horton's note. "They were on the kitchen table, along with this."

Her eyes brightened for an instant when she saw his handwriting and then darkened again as she read the note.

"He knew, didn't he?" she said.

"I think so."

"You know how else I know he knew?"

"How?"

"For weeks now he'd been getting up early and having his quiet time alone, without me. Look at his Bible," she pointed to her bed stand. "It's full of notes to himself I've never seen before now. He knew he was leaving me. I'm very unhappy with him for not telling me any of this."

"Tell me the story of the first roses that Horton brought," I requested, believing I could keep her alive if I could just get her talking about her favorite subject. "Remember we were interrupted that day I visited you in your rose garden and you never did get around to telling me how roses on Wednesday got started."

"You don't want to hear that. It's nothing, really."

"Yes, I do. From the beginning, please."

Edna sighed and closed her eyes. For a minute I thought she was going to shut the door on me. Then suddenly she spoke: "You remember how Horton was dating one of my sorority sisters at USC? She went on a summer trip and asked me to 'take care of Horton.' That was a big mistake."

"Big mistake," I repeated, noticing some color returning to her cheeks.

"We knew so much about each other right away, but his mother didn't like me. She was very controlling."

"Why didn't she like you?"

"My faith, mostly. She didn't care for God. I think she was actually threatened by people of faith because deep down she knew God was there but didn't want to accept that. Poor Horton was torn. He was her only child, and since his father had recently died, he felt compelled to care for her. I didn't see him for three years. And then suddenly, just like that, he showed up on my doorstep. We embraced and it was all over."

"And when did the roses start coming?"

"Oh, right away. The first time I asked what the occasion was, and he merely said, 'It's Wednesday.'" With that she looked at the note, on which Horton had written those same words, and the story had to stop for a while. Then she handed me the note.

"You keep it."

"Oh, Edna, I couldn't. This is the last thing he—"

"Keep it!" she said angrily. "I don't need it anymore. It's your story now."

I tried to steer her back to her memories because I could tell it was doing her good. Her anger was a good sign. "Did he bring them the next week?"

"Yes, he did. That, I thought, was pretty special."

"And what did you think the third week?"

"I'm sure I was glowing."

"Why Wednesday?" This part I already knew, and I loved it the best.

"He always told me that Wednesday with me was not just a day to get you one day closer to the weekend, it was simply a phenomenal day."

It seems like such a little thing—roses on Wednesday. I've been on and off with it since I first heard the story—mostly off. But that's just it. In forty years, Horton never missed a Wednesday.

CHAPTER SEVENTEEN
LOVE IS A ROSE

Have you ever had one of those days when you cannot consume enough coffee to prop the eyelids open and you require elbows, like crutches on the table, to hold you up?

I was having one of those days.

My mind drifted from one thought to another. They were all random notions—disconnected brain waves like streams of consciousness.

I was sitting at the counter of a roadside diner early in the morning. I would catch a plane home later that morning but I got up early enough to visit with a friend who worked in this diner. I wouldn't have had a chance to see her otherwise—her time was filled working the two jobs it took her to support herself and two children. Meeting her here was a kind of compromise, counting on some midmorning downtime for us to chat.

The diner was the kind of place that still had a jukebox. All you needed was a quarter to play three tunes. Today, however, someone had loaded the thing with quarters and punched in the same tune over and over. It was Linda Ronstadt's "Love Is a Rose." It was a shame because I used to like this song, but if I hear it one more time. . . .

The steam from my cup promised that the coffee was hot, just the way I like it. This was diner coffee—a whole different thing from Starbucks, but still worthy in its own right. This coffee was part of the experience—the thick heavy cups, the chrome edge on the counter, the red vinyl stools, and the smell of bacon and eggs on the grill. A fine gourmet coffee wouldn't have worked here. It would have been out of character.

In front of me on the counter was a small juice glass filled with water for a rose that I figured was from someone's garden. The rose rested against the glass's brim. Like me, it needed something to hold it up.

The rose is an odd mismatch of beauty and pain, and yet God blends the two together in the same flower. This cannot be a mistake—an oversight along the production line of Creation. Roses are meant to be this way—entangling magnificence and delicacy amongst the thorns, providing no protection for those who would dare touch carelessly. I examined the rose in the glass more closely.

Ouch! No wonder the rose is the supreme metaphor for love. Love is not without injury.

"If you can't handle the beauty of a rose because of the thorns," I wrote in my notepad, noticing a little blood on my pad of paper, "you can never expect to hold a woman."

It was a bit melodramatic, but it was inspired by the warning that Linda belted out one more time: "Love is a rose, but you better not pick it. It only grows when it's on the vine. A handful of thorns and you'll know you've missed it; you lose your love when you say the word 'mine.'"

"I don't think even Neil Young would like hearing his own song this many times." It was my friend, Kate, topping my coffee off even though I'd only had a few sips.

"No kidding. That's a Neil Young song? Who keeps playing it, anyway?" I asked.

"It's that guy over there in the corner booth. He comes in once in a while and always plays the death out of that song."

"He probably said 'Mine.'"

"Yep, and all he's got now is a handful of thorns."

"I love places like this where you can figure out everyone's life."

"Wish someone would figure out mine," she said as a new party came in the door. Kate hurried over to seat them, leaving me to reflect on the metaphor.

Linda—Neil Young, whoever—is talking about a different kind of rose than what comes to mind when I think about women. I think about the roses that are grown for me to purchase as a prize for the woman of my affections or to brighten up life like those roses on Wednesday that I remember on occasion. Or the rose could even be a woman, plucked from the garden of other flowers to be my possession. But Linda sings about something else. She describes the rose as a woman growing in a garden. She would have me tend to this flower, not pick it. I like this use of the metaphor, though I have grasped so little of what it means. I think it means that I cultivate the soil, water the plant, weed it, and get scratched in the process. I don't "pick" the woman's beauty. I don't cut her off at the stem and put her on display. I come to the garden where she is growing and appreciate her as a source of life, and I contribute to that life if I can.

I leaned in to see if I could smell the rose in front of me and a familiar voice said, "A rose by any other name would smell as sweet."

"Shakespeare?" I asked, turning around.

Kate nodded. "*Romeo and Juliet*. Love is such a tragedy."

I knew that there was a lot behind that statement for Kate. Her life held much tragedy, and yet there was a careless optimism about her as well. Kate walked around as if she had some kind of secret that made her brim with joy inside, but I also had a feeling no one was going to find out what that was unless he qualified.

"So what are we having this morning?" Kate's tightly curled, fine hair gave her a spunky look, despite her pain. There was an unmistakable playfulness in her smoke blue eyes.

"Coffee's okay for right now, except I probably should get something in my stomach. Do you have muffins or something like that?"

"We make our own coffee cake here. It's scrumptious."

"Say no more."

When Kate returned with my order, she sat on the stool next to mine, using only one of her elbows to prop herself up. She was more awake than I. She stared at me as I dug into the coffee cake. The moment of silence made me a little uncomfortable. "What do you want to talk about?" she finally asked.

My first thought was to talk about roses, but opting for self-protection I blurted out instead: "Why isn't a fine woman like you not married, Kate?" She seemed surprised.

"You just used a double negative."

"Did I?" stumbling over my words. "I guess I did."

"Aren't you a bit too old to be asking me a question like that?" she said, her eyes dancing. She was toying with me as I tried to squirm my way out of a dumb question. Finally she had mercy on me and answered, her tone suddenly much more serious.

"When my husband left me twelve years ago, I ran around in horror, realizing for the first time as a mother that I couldn't make things right. If I were a mother lion I could devour the enemy, drag the cubs into the cave, and lick their wounds—sorry, I fell asleep last night watching Animal Planet—but my cubs were out in the elements, developing at the wrong pace.

"He left me with no house, no car, no job, two very small children, and no alimony. Well, actually I was awarded it but never received it," she said, as if inhaling the cold, hard truth one more time and then releasing it. She continued, "One thing he did leave me, though . . ."

"What's that?" I asked, hoping for some better news from my gender's side of things.

"Two sexually transmitted diseases."

"Kate! How am I to respond to that?" I quickly deferred to the 'American Beauty' sleeping in the orange-juice glass of water in front of me. "Very pretty."

"Thanks, it's from my garden, my hiding place. You should have seen the rose garden I tended while I lived on my father's farm. That's where I took my children after my husband left. I was so pumped to prove myself that I tarred the roof, fixed the fence, sharecropped, raised livestock, and still had time for a rose garden. It was my link to the ground—to something real I could trust. Like the link that occurred when Jesus stood before me and I saw Him for the first time and turned over my heart. Then love flowed out of His wounds into my wounds and I knew, I knew, I knew this was His plan. Jesus is the ultimate link, but there are many other links in our passage here. I think He wants us to become aware of those links, like you and me, as well."

"You are as articulate in person as you are in your

e-mails," I said. Kate was the first person I had met in person after first meeting online. She had responded to a piece I wrote on how Christians are such bad tippers with a ream of firsthand experiences to confirm my observation. She had educated me on how their bad example hinders her relationships with coworkers who are not Christians. We had become friends over the last few years, and her e-mails were all publishable material.

Compliments aside, I found that this conversation was suddenly making me uncomfortable. Did I want to be linked to a single mom? a waitress in a funky diner? And why did I want to keep her small and insignificant right now? Why was I surprised that a waitress at a two-bit coffee shop was so articulate and well-read? Suddenly I recalled the numerous times my wife had mentioned how men hold women as either above them (like their mother and in some cases their wife) or below them (like a mistress or imaginary lover). Had I made myself out to be morally better than Kate? Was she lucky that I was spending time with her, or was I the fortunate one? How difficult it was for me to accept her as she was accepting me now—as an equal.

"What happened to you and the farm? How come you're not still there?"

"I would still be there now if I could manage the work. It was weariness. You can't run the Ponderosa without the guys. But I still have a rose garden, even with my little house."

Kate's eyes suddenly showed her fatigue, and I

wondered how she managed to take care of everything. While I couldn't imagine her asking help from anyone, I couldn't help but think what it would mean to her not to be alone—to have somebody who really cared about her.

Someone called out "ma'am!" and she was off, muttering to herself something about what was the point of new name tags if no one was going to notice you had a name.

Kate left her church shortly after her divorce and stayed away for a long time because she felt she would not be accepted. Whether the slights were perceived or real, she felt judged by others. "The welcome committee" at the door of the church was not enough. "I can go to Wal-Mart for that," she said, using a classic Kate-ism.

"People look at me and think there must be something wrong with me because I am a single mom and have chosen not to marry again. They blame me for my marital status. 'Couldn't you have just hung in there a little bit longer?' they say. 'Surely, he was just going through a phase.'"

But she eventually came back to the church, partly because of a pastor who reached out to her and partly because she became confident in herself through the knowledge that she was loved by God, and it no longer mattered what people thought. That's the Kate I'm talking to right now in this diner.

When she stopped back to talk again, I asked her how things were going at church, and she broke into a little laugh. "Oh, wait till I tell you about the women's retreat."

"You went on a church women's retreat?" That seemed like quite a big step for Kate.

"Some kind soul in the church paid my way. In hindsight, grocery money would have helped more. I was the light packer—the one whose backpack didn't fit in with the matching luggage. The bus ride was horrible. They talked about their perfect husbands, perfect children, white picket fences, and they sang choruses. It was awful.

"At the camp meeting they brought out a list of questions (as if we couldn't come up with our own). One was, 'Does anyone have a sexual problem?' Dead silence. They were all perfect but I raised my hand, and what do you think? *They laughed!* So I asked, 'Don't you think people who are not having sex are having a problem with it?' As I recall, they nodded their heads and went to the next question—something like, 'How does your husband greet you in the morning?' You get the point: Honesty is rejected. Second point: Real Christians are married. The single women should go up the Amazon as missionaries."

"Do they have a singles group at your church?"

"If they did, I wouldn't go. I need married men in my life; my children do too. It has been beneficial for us to be involved with married couples more than singles. Keeps the perspective realistic. If I had taken the 'singles group' option my children would be even more uncomfortable with their sexuality.

"Speaking of kids, want to see the latest picture of my two?" she said, setting down her coffeepot and reaching into her apron.

"I was beginning to think you'd never ask." That last part was pure sarcasm. I don't even carry pictures of my own kids with me—much less ask to see someone else's.

She showed me a picture and kept talking about her children. "Can you tell they're struggling? I watched my daughter here, a consistent B student, immediately start getting straight As after my husband left."

"What's wrong with that?" I asked.

"Nothing, unless you are not an A student, which she is not. She focused on one thing and would not let go. It was her way of denying the facts and living in illusion. She was unwilling to experience her own pain. My son fought in his own way, too, refusing to dress himself and tie his own shoes. He was six then."

It was clear that Kate wondered what price her children had paid as a result of her marriage breakdown. The guilt was all over her face. "Do they look happy? Tell me they look happy. Can you tell anything?"

"They are beautiful, Kate."

She looked adoringly at them for a minute. "I would do anything for them . . . anything." She left to check on her other customers.

Life can't be easy for Kate. The same goes for so many single mothers and their children who have held to the earth and to God for life and love for generation after generation. If not for Christ and His love, they would die. Love is never without injury.

"Okay," Kate said as she stopped by for a few more minutes. "Question of the day: Why is it that men suddenly become anonymous when you start talking about the plight of women like me? Is it because of the secrecy surrounding the 'sins of the father'? Are we protecting the 'reputation' of the man? Is there a pact you guys all sign that you won't rag on each other?"

Here we go, I thought. She had a temporary lull in traffic and obviously had been planning our next discussion.

"How come you and my wife are so famous for these kind of questions, like, 'How come you're such a jerk? Is it this reason or that?' Doesn't give me too many pleasant options."

"Probably because you are," she said with a wink.

But there have been vast changes in social norms over recent years, and I believe John Wayne is back on the trail, wanting to take back what many men perceive the feminist movement took away. Do we encourage each other to be irresponsible just so women can assume all men will be unsupportive? Let's not have anybody break the code here. Is this a device we have made up by which isolation is our solution?

Ah, isolation. I love it; just my thoughts and me. On the road again . . . going anywhere (going nowhere).

"Isolation is bad for any of us," Kate broke in, as if reading my thoughts. "I can tell you that isolation squeezes the walls of the house in." And then, surprisingly, she launched into a confession of her own, saying that she had avoided responsibilities as a single mom the way a man would if there were one around. "Lack of finances is part of it, but even greater is the exhaustion from wearing so many hats. Single mothers plain and simple wear out.

"One evening when my kids were at peak hormone level, the back child-support amount had reached twelve thousand dollars, and I was in need of another root canal, my daughter came to me asking for money for a yearbook, and when I told her 'not possible at this time,' her heart caved in. I went to my room because I was exhausted, turned up the music and blocked it out, and then it hit me: The isolation was working against me, and I was reacting the way my husband would have. I was shutting down, retreating, going inside, and not talking.

"Isolation as a single parent works against me. I need to know I am doing a good job. I need to be rebuked when I am selfish. I need to be corrected and supported if I'm going to be softened. I have retreated when I should have hugged. When the burdens of a family are placed on a woman, we begin to respond by retreating, shutting down. It's easier than dealing with a suitcase of emotion. I know God did not design the family to be like this."

Recognizing the loss of Kate's self-respect and her sense of complete aloneness engendered a protective response in me that filtered down to my values. What actions would I take in the face of this new information? Could I duck her problems because of the miles between us? Suddenly I found images of other single moms popping into my mind, even as I tried to tell myself I only knew a few. Chalk that up to insensitivity. They weren't drawing attention to themselves; they were just going about their business, and I wasn't noticing them. Why did I rarely respond to them with Christ's heart?

There must be a garden of stories written on the heart of every single mother and told through her life. These women's stories echo in my mind—a confusing combination of absolute courage and extreme loneliness, commitment despite unfulfilled promises, compassion in the midst of so many cold shoulders and alienation. As I scribbled out the last of what I remembered of Kate's stories, I saw, through my reflection in the juice glass, the struggle for dignity among the single women I knew, for they were in my backyard—roses neglected in my own garden.

There is a thin membrane that protects the self, and love's thorns can puncture it with ease and tear it open. This is the painful service that love provides: It strips away our protective layer, leaving us open to both hurt and love, and since we are human and fallible, we cannot love without hurting or be loved without being hurt.

When we lived in Massachusetts, I once cared for a trellis of wild roses along one side of a stone wall in front of our home. Every spring, the plants needed to be weeded. Long strands of thick, thorny flowerless shoots had to be pruned so that the smaller, blooming stems would receive all the nourishment. Those thorny shoots constantly fought me, poking through leather gloves and ripping open the plastic leaf bags I tried to contain them in. My hands were puffy for days after this ordeal, and my arms wore a road map of scratches.

It is in caring for love, as with roses, that a man experiences his deepest pain. It is man's most severe test.

In *The Scarlet Letter*, both the minister and Hester committed the sin, but only Hester wore the letter. She bore the brunt of his sin on her chest while he went free. Single mothers are often what's left of men who have given up on themselves—men who are deficient in human warmth. Their children are aware of the scarlet letter their mothers bear and of the society that helped produce it. From an early age, they are fixated on the emblem and will always carry the scars of their abandonment. Shame becomes the key ingredient in the life of these victims.

"More coffee, handsome?" Kate filled my cup before I could answer.

"Kate, you remember *The Scarlet Letter*?"

"Look on my chest."

"Well, I've been trying not to." I was mocking now.

"Oh, don't get me started on that stupid rationalization!"

"But that's exactly what I'm realizing. How we men pass the blame on to you. Like you cause me to stumble or make me lust by the way you dress or carry yourself. 'Stop being beautiful; you're making me sin!'"

Kate rolled her eyes. "What brings this on?"

"Well, I'm confessing to you that I'm the guy. I'm that minister guy in the story, what's his name?"

"Dimmesdale? Reverend Arthur Dimmesdale?"

"Yeah, that guy. I'm Reverend Dimmesdale. I have put

you down in order that I might feel superior and not have to look at my own sin."

"Well, honey, don't be too hard on yourself. We're all sinners." Then she took my hand in hers and said, "Focus on love, forgiveness, and hope. That will overcome your fears. You've got it inside you." I winced internally as I realized how hard it was for me to receive counsel from her. I had to fight off the tendency to defend myself. My wounded ego was trying hard to jump back up on top again.

Suddenly, as if on cue, someone picked "Love Is a Rose" on the jukebox, and we both laughed out loud.

"Laugh with us sinners," Kate said as she gained control of herself. "Just listen to your friend, you'll enjoy laughing at yourself, and trust the Lord to do the rest. That's all you have to do."

CHAPTER EIGHTEEN
MICHAEL DOUGLAS
AND ME

When my second son was born in 1999, the only guy
I knew about who was a new father and older than me
was Michael Douglas. And he had a new, young wife as
his excuse. What was mine? Twenty-six years into my
first and only marriage, with two kids off to college, and
I was changing diapers again? *Which way do these flaps go
anyway? Neither side seems sticky. Well, would you look at
that? Flaps down and the kid is strapped for poop.*

Six months into the new life of our second son and
third child, I noticed a sharp pain developing in my wrist.
When it started to interfere with my work, I decided

to go see the doctor. He took one look and knew exactly what it was; he was just a little puzzled as to how I had gotten it.

"We normally see this kind of problem in new mothers. It's from lifting the baby," he gestured. "It's a type of tendonitis we call, 'new baby wrist.' You been lifting anything lately?"

"Yes, Doc. My new baby."

I walked out with a shot of cortisone in my new baby wrist and wondered what might be next. Old dad back? Grandpa knee? It's true; I have noticed a significant reduction in my endurance for horsy rides this time around. The nerves in my knees seem more raw than I remember.

Some days I can't believe I'm doing this, and yet that feeling does not in any way equal regret. It's more of a sanity issue. I feel like Steve Martin in *Father of the Bride Part II*, adding up how old I will be at various stages in my son's growth, and how we can save money at the movies. "One child, two seniors, please . . ."

Most people my age are talking empty nest. Our nest was empty for all of two weeks. My second child went off to college in late August. My third was born two weeks later—September 9, 1999, to be exact. That's a 9/9/99 baby: something special.

It began at a lunch meeting with my wife and a pregnant twenty-one-year-old who was three months away from delivery. She was there to see if my wife was really serious about her offer to adopt the baby. I was there to see if I could possibly support such a thing.

We'd been at this place before, only not quite this far along. My wife had always wanted more children. I hadn't. Now in our early fifties, I could breathe easier. Time had turned this disagreement into a nonissue, or so I thought.

I knew my wife often did all she could to support women who had decided not to choose abortion. I had heard her say many times that she would care for anyone's baby if the mother would be willing to have it. I knew all this; I just never thought someone would actually take her up on it. Now that someone was sitting across the table from me all bright and blooming from the life growing within her.

That had been my first surprise. I think I went in expecting someone in trouble—unsure of herself and embarrassed, someone who needed to be rescued. But looking at her through the eyes of my wife, I saw the noble woman she had told me about. I didn't see some-one ashamed and desperate. I saw someone very brave and gloriously pregnant.

"Come over here," she said, taking my hand when I got there and placing it on her tummy. "Feel that?" Yes, I felt it. Like Thomas the doubter with his hand on the Lord's side, I felt new life.

At times like this you start looking for answers—resources to provide hope in a bad situation. Certainly someone would step up, some other couple, an agency. We could help her find some of these resources, and this lunch would soon be over. A cup of coffee and we'd be on our way.

But that didn't happen. Instead, a heightening sense of protectiveness welled up inside me. This woman was having a baby she was asking me to care for, and I knew I would give this child the best possible chance in the world. It was not an entirely logical feeling, because I'm sure there were others who could do this as well as my wife and I. But I could not guarantee her any other option.

I'm not sure at what point I knew this was right, but sometime during that lunch meeting the starch went out of my shirt, and I turned from skeptic to expectant dad.

Here it was right before me: a chance to do something more than just be pro-life—an eighteen-year, $300,000 chance (the latest estimate I read of how much it costs to raise a child).

It suddenly dawned on me that this boy growing in her was our son. I knew it as strongly as if my wife had announced her pregnancy, Sarah-like, laughing out loud in the kitchen while I entertained angels in the next room.

And today I watch this little guy, all of four years, racing around with the cocky air of a kid who knows he's somebody—knows he's loved, knows he's special, knows that his little four-year-old discoveries count.

When I look into his eyes I see someone who has always belonged to me. Every time I look at him I am flooded with thankfulness that God would grace us in this way. Up until his birth, I thought we were doing him, God, and the world a favor. Now I realize we are the ones upon whom the favor has been bestowed.

I get it now. I get it so much more than I did twenty years ago with my first two children. I get the value of life. I get the importance of those moments spent with total concentration on the activity and thought processes of a child. I get it that a child returns to us the meaning of the moments in our life. A child only knows here and now. God watches our life and personality unfold before Him with the same satisfaction that I get as I watch my son grow. Yes, there is much to bring God sorrow in the world, and yet there is much that brings Him joy. I'm convinced of this, or else He would not have bothered with us in the first place. He wants us to have a heightened awareness of this human experience He created.

So I take more time now being a father than I did twenty years ago. I notice more. I have much more patience. It's not that I have more time; it's that I have more reasons to make time. I endure my son's temper tantrums without taking it personally. I don't consider any time with him mundane or wasted. I know he's learning every minute. He doesn't miss a thing. I don't want to either.

There's something to this Michael Douglas–Catherine Zeta-Jones thing. Like Michael, I may be in a wheelchair when I watch my son graduate, but he's going to have to deal with the fact that he has the best dad he could have possibly had. This dad chose him like the Father chose us, willing to endure anything—willing to pay the price, even knowing what the price would be. This dad didn't stare through a maternity window at the wiggling consequence of his feverish trip down the aisle and wonder how he got himself into this.

This dad knew what he was doing from the beginning. And it won't matter whether or not my son ever appreciates it. I will.

I already do.

CHAPTER NINETEEN
FORM FOLLOWS
(DYS)FUNCTION

As a creature of habit, I drink my coffee at home from one of two different cups. Early in the morning during the week I use my Starbucks stainless-steel mug with the snap-on lid and black handle. It has an air chamber built into it that keeps the coffee hot almost as well as a thermos would. It's dented in a couple of places from the number of times it has been dropped, and the rubber handle is beginning to get a little sticky from going through the dishwasher almost every day for at least three years. Nevertheless, I am resolved to keeping this mug in service and won't easily part with something that has become, in essence, an extension of my arm.

But on those lazy Saturday mornings when I am not

on the road, the utility mug remains in the kitchen cabinet while a finer, more fashionable cup takes its place. This cup is one of four whimsical terra-cotta cups that are all different in size, shape, and thickness, with saucers so eccentric in appearance that only my wife would seek out and impulsively acquire them.

Watching her purchase peculiar items such as these cups and saucers distresses me to no end. Her choices can be so impractical. There's no way around it; these cups and saucers are dysfunctional. The cups tilt slightly one way or another, and depending on how you set them down, they can rock a little and even tip over.

Now I do not want to imply that my wife and her choices are completely unreasonable. She recognizes the need for useful items; it is just that she sees everything from a completely different perspective than I do. I grew up learning the rule that "form follows function," with the bottom line of this principle being the more something is designed to function right, the more beautiful it will be by necessity (i.e., a comfortable shoe will be a beautiful shoe because of its comfort).

My wife, on the other hand, challenges this understanding through her engaging ability to help me look in a different way at things that I have always thought were obvious. Of course, her perspective is as obvious to her as mine is to me. But to me this is reinventing the rules; it's unconventional and very uncomfortable. She takes leaps in lateral thinking, while I prefer to move forward in a sequential order—like *form follows function.*

I admit, however, when I can get over my own barriers, her process is always revealing and invariably leads to further understanding. So while the cool hand of reason rules a good portion of the week, on Saturday mornings form follows (dys)function, as I have not only learned to drink but have actually come to appreciate drinking from dysfunctional coffee cups.

For some time my wife had these cups and saucers all in a row on the windowsill in the kitchen just because she liked looking at them. That's when I quietly judged them as works of art and not functional coffee cups. But that was before I started using them. Why I started using them, I cannot rationally say. Maybe Marti's lateral thinking is starting to have an effect on me, but they just looked as if coffee served out of them would taste good, and I found out that it did.

However, as useful cups, they have not held up well. We still have all four saucers left, but two cups are gone and the two that remain have lost their handle. The handles were especially vulnerable, comically twisted into various shapes from the bottom of the cup to the top.

Still, I like using the cups on weekends, even though I have spilled my coffee numerous times because I did not place the cup solidly on its saucer. You might wonder why I keep using them, given the somewhat frustrating experience with these cups.

Well, I do not know whether there is any truth to it—some interaction between the molecules of liquid and their container—but coffee tastes different in those crazy cups. I have found Styrofoam to be the worst and will go to great length to avoid it. Paper, if it's Starbucks or an equivalent, is okay. Mugs and cups vary. The blue idiosyncratic pottery my wife purchased, however, is perfect for my taste. Practically speaking, the cups are quite small, necessitating frequent refills; I don't mind this because that means the coffee will stay naturally hot. I can drink a cup before it has a chance to cool down. And I use them on the weekend when I can afford the luxury of fussing with this.

So here I am, at peace with the inconvenience of drinking out of a small cup that has no handle, that gets too hot to hold, that I cannot set down without the danger of spilling the coffee, and that I have to balance gingerly with one hand while I manage a muffin with the other, meaning I have to set one of them down to turn the newspaper page.

Who else would do this? Only someone as dysfunctional as I am, who has also come to appreciate the strangely beautiful things in life. Even things like me. I tip. I rock on my base. I fall over and spill out. I cannot be held for very long without burning someone. Nevertheless, I am seen as lovely and passionate by some, and good to drink from. I was made this way by the Creator who had an eye for those of us who tip over and do not function just to sit perfectly on a windowsill. He has found a way to use me regardless of my broken handles and uneven stance.

Though we no longer have a complete set, Marti

would never think of throwing away what remains. She thinks what is left is still pleasant to the eye. I'm glad she does, because the coffee still tastes good out of them. These pieces are not replaceable. They are one of a kind, just as you are . . . and just as I am.

So I'm holding my coffee cup this morning in the palm of my hand. The cup is hot, almost to the point of burning, but I can handle it. The newspaper is telling me about a world that I am slowly waking to as the caffeine works its way into my brain. In the paper is a story about how experts have discovered that coffee, especially when consumed daily in large quantities, can be beneficial in preventing certain kinds of cancer and diabetes.

I knew that all along.

NOTES

1. John Ortberg, *Love Beyond Reason* (Grand Rapids, Mich.: Zondervan, 1998), 16.
2. *New Yorker* (April 22–29, 2002): 72.
3. From the album *Crowded House*, copyright © 1986 Roundhead Music (BMI).
4. Fred Rogers, *The World According to Mister Rogers* (New York: Hyperion Press, 2003), 184.
5. Ibid., 53.
6. This information was obtained from PACE ministry (Post Abortion Counseling and Education), Perimeter Church, Duluth, Atlanta.

Free Discussion Guide for **Confessions of a Caffeinated Christian***!*
A discussion guide written by
John Fischer is available at

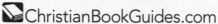

ChristianBookGuides.com

SaltRiver Books are a bit like saltwater: buoyant; sometimes stinging; a mixture of sweet and bitter, just like real life. These books are intelligent, thoughtful, and finely crafted—but not pretentious, condescending, or out of reach. They take on real life from a Christian perspective. Look for SaltRiver Books, an imprint of Tyndale House Publishers, everywhere Christian books are sold.

Intelligent. Thought-provoking. Authentic.

w w w . s a l t r i v e r b o o k s . c o m

DATE DUE

		ISSCW B	
		F529	
FISCHER, JOHN			
CONFESSIONS OF A			
CAFFEINATED CHRISTIAN			
CENTRAL LIBRARY			
12/05			